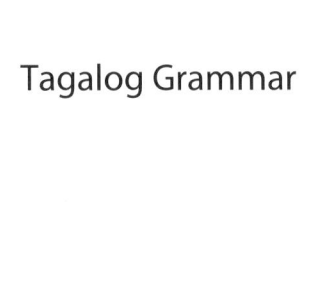

# Tagalog Grammar

# Tagalog Grammar

A Typological Perspective

Takanori Hirano

HITUZI SYOBO

Copyright © Takanori Hirano 2012
First published 2012

Author: Takanori Hirano


All rights reserved. Except for the quotation of short passages for the purposes of criticism and review, no part of this publication may be reproduced, stored in a retrieval system, or transmitted in any form or by any means, electronic, mechanical, photocopying, recording or otherwise, without the written prior permission of the publisher.
In case of photocopying and electronic copying and retrieval from network personally, permission will be given on receipts of payment and making inquiries. For details please contact us through e-mail. Our e-mail address is given below.


Book Design © Eber

Hituzi Syobo Publishing
Yamato bldg. 2F, 2-1-2 Sengoku Bunkyo-ku Tokyo, Japan
112-0011

phone +81-3-5319-4916  fax +81-3-5319-4917
e-mail: toiawase@hituzi.co.jp
http://www.hituzi.co.jp/
postal transfer 00120-8-142852

ISBN 978-4-89476-549-8
Printed in Japan

# Preface

This book aims to describe the structure of Tagalog with a focus on typological characterization, which I believe will contribute further to the development of Philippine linguistics, and of linguistic typology in general. This is because there is no good book on Tagalog from a typological perspective, despite the fact that the literature on linguistic typology often illustrates examples from the language.

This book has been written for students of linguistics both inside and outside Japan with a prior knowledge of linguistics and typology. In order for readers to have a better understanding of the meanings of illustrative sentences, a word or morpheme is repeatedly glossed, which will also help them to increase their vocabulary.

Special thanks go to the following people, without whose assistance I could not have carried out this project: Ms Cyril A. Furuya (born in Manila in 1964, a graduate of the University of Santo Tomas (UST)), Ms Maria Khristina S. Manueli (born in Manila in 1977, Associate Professor at the University of the Philippines (UP)) and Ms Maria Fatima Bautista (born in Batangas in 1985) as my language consultants, Professor Irma Peneyra, my Tagalog teacher when I was a student at UP from June 1974 to September 1975, Professor Viveca Hernandez, my mentor when I stayed at UP in 2003, and Ernesto A. Constantino, Professor Emeritus at UP.

Data were also taken and adapted from Aspillera (1969, abbreviated as [BT]), Ramos (1971a, [TD]), Ramos (1971b, [TS]), Ramos and Cena (1990, [MT]), English (1977, 1986) and others. This book also includes my own illustrative examples. Unless otherwise noted, data are taken and adapted from Ms Furuya and Ms Manueli. Data given by Ms Manuel were particularly useful in writing the following chapters: 'The prefix *ma-*', 'Ability/Permission', 'Auxiliary-like verbs', 'Adverbs', 'Subjectless sentences', 'Conjunctions', 'Verbal affixes' and 'Nominal and adjectival affixes'.

A word must be said about the structure of this book. The book can be divided into four parts: Part I Words and Sentences (Chapters 3–9), Part II Verbs and Morphology (Chapters 10–16), Part III Particles (Chapters 17–21) and Part IV Miscellaneous (Chapters 22–29).

The publication of this book is supported in part by a Grant-in-Aid for publication of Scientific Result (No. 235076) of the Japan Society for the Promotion of Science.

Finally, I am grateful to Ms Danica Salazar for her excellent proofreading.

# Contents

Preface v
Abbreviations xix

## Chapter 1  Introduction 1
1.1. Filipino or Tagalog 1
1.2. Stress 2
1.3. Description of morphosyntax 3

## Chapter 2  Phonology 5
2.1. Vowels 5
2.2. /e/ and /o/ 6
   2.2.1. External development 6
   2.2.2. Internal development 6
2.3. Consonants 8
   2.3.1. Glottal stop 8
   2.3.2. /d/ and /r/ 9
   2.3.3. dy [ʤ], ts [ʧ] and siyV [ʃiyV] 9
   2.3.4. Syllable structure 10
2.4. Prosody 10
2.5. Borrowed words 11
2.6. Stress rules 11

## Part I  Words and Sentences    15

## Chapter 3    Typological characteristics of Tagalog    17
3.1.  Introduction    17
3.2.  Verb-initial language    17
    3.2.1.  Voice    19
    3.2.2.  Tense and aspect    23
    3.2.3.  How to gloss the aspects    24
3.3.  Is Tagalog morphologically ergative or accusative?    25

## Chapter 4    Sentence types    29
4.1.  Unmarked and marked constructions    29
4.2.  Unmarked constructions    30
    4.2.1.  Situational sentences    30
    4.2.2.  Indefinite and definite sentences    32
    4.2.3.  Possessives    33
4.3.  Marked constructions    34
    4.3.1.  Noun + Clause type    34
    4.3.2.  Gusto-construction    35
    4.3.3.  Existential    36
    4.3.4.  Subjectless sentences    37

## Chapter 5    The particle *ang*    39

## Chapter 6    Nouns and verbs in Tagalog    43

## Chapter 7  Categorization of words in Tagalog         47
7.1.  How can root words in Tagalog be categorized?      47
7.2.  Root words and affixes                             48
7.3.  The Independence hierarchy                         49

## Chapter 8  Linker                                     53
8.1.  Introduction                                       53
8.2.  Uses of the linker                                 53
   8.2.1.  Adjective + Noun or Noun + Adjective    53
   8.2.2.  Noun + Noun                              55
   8.2.3.  Adjective_i + Adjective_j                56
8.3.  Complementizer: that in English                    57
8.4.  Other uses of the linker                           58
   8.4.1.  Demonstrative pronoun + noun             58
   8.4.2.  Sentential adverbs/adjectives            58
   8.4.3.  Auxiliary-like verbs + sentence          59
   8.4.4.  The linker *na* to make word boundaries clear  59
8.5.  Uses of the linker: summary                        59

## Chapter 9  Relative clause constructions              63
9.1.  Introduction                                       63
9.2.  Structure of relative clause constructions         63
9.3.  Subject-sensitive relative clause formation        65
9.4.  Order of relative clause and head                  66
9.5.  Special types of relative clause construction      68
   9.5.1.  Possessive relativization                68
   9.5.2.  Apposition                               69
   9.5.3.  Relative adverbs                         70

9.5.4. Head internal relative clause constructions — 70

# Part II Verbs and Morphology — 71

## Chapter 10 Agent voice 1: *-um-* verbs — 73
10.1. What is the agent voice? — 73
10.2. Conjugation pattern of -um- verbs — 74
10.3. Description of aspectual features — 76
10.4. Uses of neutral forms — 78
10.5. Accentuation of -um- verbs — 78

## Chapter 11 Agent voice 2: *mag-* verbs — 81
11.1. Agent-voiced: mag- verbs — 81
11.2. Conjugation pattern of mag- verbs — 82
11.3. Accentuation of mag- verbs — 83

## Chapter 12 Patient voice: *-(h)in* — 85
12.1. What is the patient voice? — 85
12.2. Conjugation pattern of -(h)in verbs — 88
12.3. Accentuation of -(h)in verbs — 89

## Chapter 13 Directional voice: *-(h)an* — 91
13.1. Introduction — 91
13.1.1. Locative — 91
13.1.2. Source — 92
13.1.3. Directional — 93
13.1.4. Recipient/Benefactive — 94

| | | |
|---|---|---|
| 13.1.5. | A note on the preposition *sa* | 95 |
| 13.2. | Special use of -(h)an verbs: Patient | 97 |
| 13.3. | Conjugation pattern of -(h)an verbs | 98 |
| 13.4. | Additional notes on the conjugation pattern of -(h)an verbs | 99 |
| 13.5. | Accentuation of -(h)an verbs | 100 |

## Chapter 14  The accusative/ergative controversy 101
| | | |
|---|---|---|
| 14.1. | Introduction | 101 |
| 14.2. | Accusative and ergative morphology | 101 |
| 14.3. | Problems with the ergative analysis | 103 |
| 14.3.1. | How to treat the non-subject patient marker *ng* and the directional marker *sa* | 103 |
| 14.3.2. | Two types of *ng* | 105 |
| 14.3.3. | Intransitive DV constructions | 106 |
| 14.4. | Conclusion | 107 |

## Chapter 15  Benefactive/Patient/Instrumental voice: *i-* verbs 109
| | | |
|---|---|---|
| 15.1. | Introduction | 109 |
| 15.2. | Benefactive | 109 |
| 15.2.1. | i- verbs: related to root words affixed by -um- | 109 |
| 15.2.2. | ipag- verbs: related to root words affixed by mag- | 110 |
| 15.3. | Patient: related to root words affixed by mag- | 111 |
| 15.4. | Instrumental | 113 |
| 15.5. | Conjugation pattern | 114 |
| 15.6. | Accentuation of i- verbs | 114 |

## Chapter 16 The prefix *ma-*   115
16.1. Introduction   115
16.2. Adjectival $ma_1$-   116
16.3. $ma_2$-: unergative, voluntary   117
16.4. $ma_3$-: unaccusative, involuntary   117
16.5. $ma_4$-: (in)voluntary   118
16.6. $ma_5$-: transitive verbs (voluntary action)   119
16.7. $ma_6$-: transitive (involuntary event)   120
16.8. $ma_7$-: intransitive/transitive (involuntary action)   120
16.9. The prefix *ma-* and morphological ergativity   121

## Part III Particles   123

## Chapter 17 Topic marker: *ay*   125
17.1. Predicate + Subject order   125
17.2. Subject + ay + Predicate order   126
17.3. Sentential topics and the topic marker ay   127
17.4. Adverbial topics   129
17.5. Subject and topic   130
   17.5.1. The connective *ay*   130
   17.5.2. Double-subject constructions   131
17.6. The subject/topic hierarchy   132

## Chapter 18 Question marker *ba*   133
18.1. Yes-no questions   133
18.2. *Wh-*questions   136
18.3. Position of the question marker *ba*   138

| | | |
|---|---|---|
| 18.3.1. | The number of syllables: agent pronouns | 138 |
| 18.3.2. | *Wh*-questions and subject pronouns | 139 |
| 18.3.3. | *Ay* sentences and *ba* | 140 |
| 18.4. | Responses to yes-no questions | 140 |
| 18.5. | Responses to negative questions | 142 |
| 18.6. | Positions of the question marker across languages | 143 |

## Chapter 19   Negation: *hindî* 145
| | | |
|---|---|---|
| 19.1. | Negative sentence formation | 145 |
| 19.2. | Examples | 145 |
| 19.2.1. | *Hindî* + PRED + NP: SUBJ | 145 |
| 19.2.2. | *Hindî* + PRN: SUBJ + PRED | 146 |
| 19.3. | Use of *hindî* in the *ay*-sentences | 147 |

## Chapter 20   Case marking 149
| | | |
|---|---|---|
| 20.1. | Common nouns | 149 |
| 20.2. | Demonstratives | 150 |
| 20.3. | Human proper nouns | 153 |
| 20.4. | Personal pronouns | 154 |
| 20.5. | Further discussion | 156 |
| 20.5.1. | Evidence that Tagalog lacks the *ng-P* form for definite nouns | 156 |
| 20.5.2. | Causative constructions | 157 |

## Chapter 21   The particle *sa*: the syntax/semantics continuum 161
| | | |
|---|---|---|
| 21.1. | Introduction | 161 |
| 21.2. | Dative | 161 |
| 21.2.1. | Recipient | 162 |

| | |
|---|---|
| 21.2.2. Causee | 162 |
| 21.3. Other functions | 162 |
| 21.3.1. Locative | 162 |
| 21.3.2. Directional | 163 |
| 21.3.3. Time | 164 |
| 21.3.4. Cause | 164 |
| 21.3.5. Comitative | 164 |
| 21.4. Tagalog *sa* and Japanese *ni* compared | 165 |
| 21.4.1. Dative | 165 |
| 21.4.2. Locative | 165 |
| 21.4.3. Time | 166 |
| 21.4.4. Directional | 166 |

## Part IV  Miscellaneous 167

## Chapter 22  Ability/Permission 169

| | |
|---|---|
| 22.1. Introduction | 169 |
| 22.2. Ability | 170 |
| 22.3. Permission | 172 |
| 22.4. Prohibition | 173 |
| 22.5. Conjugation of *maka-* verbs | 174 |
| 22.6. Stative: *naka-* | 175 |

## Chapter 23  Auxiliary-like verbs 177

| | |
|---|---|
| 23.1. Introduction | 177 |
| 23.2. Examples | 177 |
| 23.2.1. *gustó*: like | 177 |
| 23.2.2. *kailángan* : need | 179 |

| | | |
|---|---|---|
| 23.2.3. | *dápat* : must, should | 179 |
| 23.2.4. | *maaári'*: may, allowed | 180 |
| 23.2.5. | *puwéde*: may, permitted | 180 |
| 23.2.6. | *hindí' puwéde*: not allowed | 181 |

## Chapter 24    Adverbs                                              183
| | | |
|---|---|---|
| 24.1. | Introduction | 183 |
| 24.2. | Examples of sentential-adverbs/nang-adverbs | 184 |
| 24.3. | Examples of sentential adverbs/*nang-adverb | 185 |
| 24.4. | Interchangeability | 186 |
| 24.5. | Structures of sentential adverbs and related constructions | 187 |

## Chapter 25    Existentials and possessives: *may*                  189
| | | |
|---|---|---|
| 25.1. | Introduction | 189 |
| 25.2. | The *may* form | 190 |
| 25.3. | The *mayroón* form | 191 |
| 25.4. | The *walá'* form | 192 |

## Chapter 26    Subjectless sentences                                193
| | | |
|---|---|---|
| 26.1. | Introduction | 193 |
| 26.2. | Subjectless sentences: examples | 194 |
| 26.2.1. | Meteorology | 194 |
| 26.2.2. | Darkness/brightness | 195 |
| 25.2.3. | Natural phenomena | 196 |
| 26.3. | Recently finished | 196 |
| 26.4. | Exclamation | 197 |

## Chapter 27  Conjunctions — 199
27.1.  Introduction — 199
27.2.  Coordinating conjunctions — 199
    27.2.1.  *at* : and — 199
    27.2.2.  *péro, ngúnit*: but — 200
    27.2.3.  *o*: or — 200
27.3.  Subordinating conjunctions — 201
    27.3.1.  *nang, kung, kapag, noon*: when — 201
    27.3.2.  *bagamán, káhit (na)*: although — 205
    27.3.3.  *dáhil (sa)*: because (of) — 205
    27.3.4.  *samakatuwíd, kayá'*: therefore, so — 206
    27.3.5.  *káhit na*: even if — 206
    27.3.6.  *bágo*: before — 206
    27.3.7.  *pagkatápos*: after — 207

## Chapter 28  Verbal affixes — 209
28.1.  Introduction — 209
28.2.  *maki-* : request, joint/mutual action, etc. — 209
28.3.  *paki-* : request — 210
28.4.  *naka-* : stative — 212
28.5.  *(i)pa-* : causative (patient-voiced) — 213
28.6.  *papag-* : causative (causee-voiced) — 213
28.7.  *ka-* : recently finished 'just finish V-ing' — 214

## Chapter 29  Nominal and adjectival affixes — 215
29.1.  Introduction — 215
29.2.  Nominal affixes — 215
    29.2.1.  *ka-RW-an*: abstract noun — 215

| | | |
|---|---|---|
| 29.2.2. | *-(h)an*: place | 216 |
| 29.2.3. | *tag-* : related to weather or season | 217 |
| 29.2.4. | *ka-* | 217 |
| 29.2.5. | *pang-* : (used) for | 217 |
| 29.2.6. | *maN-RED*: habit or occupation | 218 |
| 29.3. | Other affixes: producing prepositional phrases | 218 |
| 29.3.1. | *taga₁-/tagapag-* : duty, assignment | 218 |
| 29.3.2. | *taga₂-*: from | 219 |

References 221
Index 225

# Abbreviations

1: first person
2: second person
3: third person
A(GT): agent
ABS: absolutive
ACC: accusative
A(DJ): adjective
ADVL: adverbializer
AP: adjective phrase
AV: agent(-)voice(d)
BEN: benefactive
BG: begun
BV: benefactive voice(d)
C: consonant
CAUS: causative
Ci: initial consonant
COMP: complementizer
COP: copula
DAT: dative
DES: desiderative
DET: determiner
DIR: directional
DV: directional voice(d)
EMP: emphasis
ERG: ergative
ET: external topic
EXC: exclamation
EXCL: exclusive
FN: finished
FP: final particle
GEN: genitive
H: head
IC: immediate constituent
IMP: imperative
IMPF: imperfective
INCL: inclusive
INCP: inceptive
INS: instrumental
IT: internal topic
ITRV: intransitive verb
IV: instrumental voice(d)
LK: linker
LOC: locative
LV: locative voice(d)
N: noun
NB: not-begun
Ng-A: ng Agent
Ng-P: ng Patient
NML: nominalizer
NOM: nominative
NP: noun phrase
NS: neutral structure
NT: neutral
NV: neutral voice
O: object
OBL: oblique
PASS: passive
P(AT): patient
PF: perfective
PL: plural
PN: personal name
POL: polite
PP: prepositional phrase
PRED: predicate
PRN: pronoun
PV: patient(-)voice(d)
Q: question
RC: relative clause
RED: reduplication
RF: recently-finished
RW: root words
S(UBJ): subject

SG: singular
SM: subject marker
STAT: stative
TM: topic marker

TOP: topic
TRV: transitive verb
UA: unaccusative
UE: unergative

UF: unfinished
US: underlying structure
V: vowel or verb
Vst: verb stem

# Chapter 1

# Introduction

## 1.1. Filipino or Tagalog

The language dealt with here is Tagalog, not Filipino, or formerly Pilipino. Filipino is somewhat different from Tagalog, although it is based on Tagalog. The reason is presumably that Filipino has been influenced by other Philippine languages such as Ilocano, Cebuano, etc.

In addition, Filipino has a lot of borrowed words from Spanish and English, such as *milk* 'milk', *libro* 'book' (which is also widely used in present-day Tagalog), *titser* 'teacher', etc. For these words, Tagalog originally has the words *gatas*, *aklat* and *guro'*, respectively. Note, however, that a critical difference between Filipino and Tagalog is found in case marking; in the agent-voiced (AV) construction, Filipino has the *ng-P* marker for human proper nouns, while Tagalog does not. To give an example, 'We are going to see Mrs Aquino tomorrow' is translated into Filipino and Tagalog as follows:

(1) Filipino: Mag-ki-kita kami ni Mrs. Aquino
AV-NB-see 2PL.EXCL.NOM PN.SG.ACC Mrs. Aquino
bukas.

tomorrow
'Mrs. Aquino is going to see us tomorrow.'
Intended: 'We are going to see Mrs Aquino tomorrow.'

( 2 ) Tagalog: a. Ma-ki-kita namin si Mrs. Aquino
**PV**-NB-see PL.EXCL.ng-A PN.SG.**NOM** Mrs. Aquino
bukas.
tomorrow
'We are going to see Mrs Aquino tomorrow.'
b.*Mag-ki-kita kami ni Mrs. Aquino
AV-NB-see 2PL.EXCL.NOM PN.SG.ACC Mrs. Aquino
bukas.
tomorrow
Intended: 'We are going to see Mrs Aquino tomorrow.'

Roughly speaking, AV and PV correspond to the active and the passive, respectively, which will be discussed in the following chapters: 10. 'Agent voice 1: *-um-* verbs', 11. 'Agent voice 2: *mag-* verbs' and 12. 'Patient voice: *-(h)in*'.

## 1.2. Stress

Stress on nouns and verb stems cannot be predicted and must be marked as in *búkas* 'tomorrow' and *bukás* 'open', while the stress on the imperfective and inceptive forms of verbs is predictable if it is marked on the verb stem. The rule-governed stress need not be marked. In a nutshell, the pattern RÉD + SŚ is accepted, while the pattern RÉD + ŚS is not (RED: reduplication, S: syllable). For more information on stress rules, see Chapter 2.

## 1.3. Description of morphosyntax

Tagalog poses an important problem for morphosyntax: is the language morphologically ergative or accusative? This has been one of the central issues in Philippine linguistics. In this book, we shall examine both accusative and ergative analyses to avoid giving the readers a theoretical bias. What is important here is to make clear why Tagalog is said to be accusative or ergative. As will be mentioned in Chapter 4, I use the symbols *ng-A* and *ng-P* for the agent NP in Non-agent-voiced (Non-AV) constructions and the patient NP in Non-patient-voiced (Non-PV) constructions respectively, in order to remain neutral between the accusative and ergative analyses. Incidentally, the form *ng* is pronounced [naŋ]. It is important to note that *ng-P* denotes an indefinite patient while *ng-A* denotes a definite and indefinite agent. The accusative analysis uses the terms *genitive* and *accusative* for ng-A and ng-P, respectively. Himmelmann (2005) treats *ng-A* and *ng-P* equally and glosses them as *genitive*. The ergative analysis, on the other hand, refers to *ng-A*, *ng-P/sa-NP* and *ang-NP* as the terms *ergative*, *oblique* and *absolutive*, respectively (see Nolasco 2005).

All in all, both the accusative and the ergative analysis have shortcomings (cf. also Foley 2008), which leads us to the conclusion that Tagalog is neither accusative nor ergative, but multi-voiced.

Thus, we gloss the forms that appear in this book as follows:

( 3 ) K-um-áin **ng** manggá ang báta'.
Ci-AV.FN-eat ng-P mango SM child
'The child ate **a** mango.'
( 4 ) K-in-áin **ng** báta' ang manggá.
Ci-PV.FN-eat ng-A child SM mango
'**The** child ate the mango.'

It is evident from (3) and (4) that *ng-P* and *ng-A* are different in definiteness; *ng-P* always designates indefinite patients while *ng-A* both definite and indefinite agents. Thus, our conclusion is that the two *ng* forms must be distinguished.

Interestingly enough, Russian uses genitive to mark unquantified patient NPs, as seen in examples (5) and (6) adapted from Moravcsik (1978: 248–249).

( 5 ) a. Cvet-y　　　　narva-li.　　　　　　　(flower = cvetok: SG.NOM)
　　　 flowers-ACC　pick-we.PAST
　　　 'We picked (the) flowers.
　　b. Cvet-ov　　　　narva-li.
　　　 flower-PL.GEN　pick-we.PAST
　　　 'We picked a lot of flowers.'
( 6 ) a. Plesni kofeëk.
　　　 pour　coffee-ACC
　　　 'Pour the coffee!'
　　b. Plesni-ka　eščë　kofejk-u.
　　　 pour-please　still　coffee-GEN
　　　 'Please pour some more coffee!'

Moravcsik himself (1978: 249) calls this phenomenon the unquantified-quantified distinction, which does not necessarily correspond to the definite-indefinite distinction. A similar situation occurs in Finnish with the accusative case 'total affection' and the partitive case 'partial affection'.

Finally, a word must be said about the particle *ang*, which is termed SM (subject marker). This serves to denote a definite reference. Thus, Reid (2002) refers to the particle *ang* as *specifying-noun*.

# Chapter 2
# Phonology

## 2.1. Vowels

Tagalog has five vowel phonemes, as shown in Table 2–1 below.

| Table 2–1: Vowels | | |
|---|---|---|
| i | | u |
| | e | o |
| | a | |

The phonemes /i/ and /u/ have positional and free variants. In word-final syllables, they are realized as [e] and [o], respectively. In present-day Tagalog, however, [i] and [e] are contrastive. The same applies to [u] and [o]. Phonological changes have been brought about by internal and external developments. For one thing, Tagalog has borrowed a lot of words from Spanish and English, which have produced minimal pairs with /i/ and /e/ on the one hand, and with /u/ and /o/ on the other. This is an external development. For another, the sequences of ay/ai and aw/au have produced /e/ and /o/, respectively, which is an internal development. Examples of each type will be illustrated in the following section.

## 2.2. /e/ and /o/

### 2.2.1. External development

( 1 ) a. mesa 'table'
     b. misa 'mass' (Ramos 1971b: 7)

( 2 ) a. oso 'bear'
     b. uso 'fad' (Ramos 1971b: 7)

Examples (1) and (2) are sufficient to illustrate these changes, although several other examples can be found.

### 2.2.2. Internal development

As mentioned in Section 1, the phonemic status of /e/ and /o/ was established internally by a process through which ay/ai and aw/au fused into /e/ and /o/, respectively. See examples (3)–(7) below.

( 3 ) a. Aywan    ko.
       unknown  1SG.ng-A
     'I don't know.'
     b. Ewan ko.

( 4 ) a. tainga 'ear'                 (*ng* is pronounced [ŋ].)
     b. tenga

( 5 ) a. kailan 'when'
     b. kelan

( 6 ) a. kaunti' 'little'

b. konti' ~ konte'

( 7 ) a. isauli' 'to return'
　　 b. isoli'

The (a) examples and the (b) examples in (3)–(7) are interchangeable, although the (b) examples are used in colloquial speech. Let us now observe the words in (8) and (9) below.

( 8 ) a. totoo　　'true'
　　 b. doon　　'there'
　　 c. manood　'to watch'

( 9 ) leeg 'neck'

Note that in the examples above, [o] and [e] appear not only in final syllables, but also in non-final syllables. It seems that they can be explained in terms of assimilation. That is, [e] and [o] in non-final syllables assimilate with [e] and [o], respectively, that appear in final syllables, as shown below.

(10) a. tutuu → tutu'u → tutu'o → tuto'o → [toto'o]
　　 b. liig → li'ig → li'eg → [le'eg]
　　　 (The forms *tutuu* and *liig* are underlying forms.)

Now consider the alternation between *mayroon* and *meroon* 'to have/exist'. *Mero'on* can be explained in terms of the process: mayruun → mayru'un → mayru'on → mayro'on → mero'on.

## 2.3. Consonants

The consonantal phonemes in Tagalog are as follows:

Table 2–2: Consonants

|  | Labial | Dental | Velar | Glottal |
|---|---|---|---|---|
| Stops | p<br>b | t<br>d | k<br>g | ʔ |
| Fricatives |  | s |  | h |
| Nasals | m | n | ŋ |  |
| Liquids |  | l, r |  |  |
| Semivowels | w | y |  |  |

More specifically, /n/ and /l/ are alveolars rather than dentals, along with /s/ and /r/. /y/ is alveo-palatal. ʔ is represented by the symbol ' and ŋ by ng in this book.

### 2.3.1. Glottal stop
(11) a. aáwit ['a'á:wit], babáe [babá:'e] ~ [babá:'i] 'woman', bituín [bitu'ín], doón [do'ón], táo [tá:'o] 'person', totoó [toto'ó] 'true', ulán ['ulán] 'rain', umúulán ['umú:'ulán] 'it is raining', úulán ['ú:'ulán] 'it will rain', ...
 b. báta' [bá:ta'] 'child', dagá' [dagá'] 'rat', hindí' [hindí']~[hindé'] 'no, not', isdá' ['isdá'] 'fish', walá' [walá'] 'nothing, none', ...

It is clear from the examples in (11a) that there are two environments where the glottal stop automatically appears, i.e. word-initially when the word begins with a vowel, and intervocalically. They are predictable and, therefore, not phonemicized. As shown by the examples in (11b), the word-final glottal stop is not predictable. This must be phonemicized. The predictability of length [:] will be discussed in Section 4. Note that the glottal stop tends to disappear phrase-internally: e.g. *Anong ginagawa mo?* ← Ano-ng g-in-a-gawa' mo? (what-LK Ci-PV-UF-do 2SG.ng-A 'What are you doing?').

### 2.3.2.  /d/ and /r/
(12) a. dumatíng [dumatíŋ] 'to arrive', dumáratíng [dumá:ratíŋ] 'is arriving', dáratíng [dá:ratíŋ] 'will be arriving', ...
  b. rádyo [rá:ʤo] 'radio', regálo [regá:lo] 'gift', reló [reló] 'watch', ...
  c. áraw ['á:raw] 'sun, day', laráwan [lará:wan] 'picture', haráp [haráp] 'front', ...
  d. madalí' [madalí'] 'easy', madulás [madulás] 'slippery', ...

As shown by the examples in (12a), the word-initial /d/ alternates with [r] when it appears intervocalically. This alternation applies sometimes within a phrase and a sentence (e.g. *Hali ka rito* 'Come here', cf. *rito* < *dito* 'here'). It is important to note that the examples in (12a) show that word-initially, Tagalog originally did not have the phoneme /r/, along with the fact that Tagalog does not have native words that begin with or end in /r/. Note, however, that the language has acquired the phoneme /r/, as illustrated in examples (12b), (12c) and (12d). Examples like *madalí'* and *madulás* consist of the adjectival prefix *ma-* and the noun. Recall that Tagalog has borrowed a lot of words from Spanish and English, which leads to the phonemic status of word-initial /r/ in present-day Tagalog.

### 2.3.3.  dy [ʤ], ts [ʧ] and siyV [ʃiyV]
(13) a. diyán~dyán [ʤá(.)n] 'there', ...
  b. dyáryo [ʤá:ryo] 'newspaper', ...

(14) a. tiyán~tyán [ʧá(.)n] 'belly', ...
  b. tsá [ʧá] 'tea', intsík ['inʧík] 'Chinese', ...

(15) siyá [ʃiyá] 's/he', siyám [ʃiyám] 'nine', ...

[ʤ] took place internally and externally. It is convenient to phenemicize [ʤ] as the sequence of /d/ and /y/. *Diyán~dyán* [ʤá(.)n] 'there' is an example of internal development. *Diyán* can be analyzed as *di* 'in, at, on, etc.' + *iyán* 'that'. Incidentally, see *di* in Indonesian, which is the preposition meaning 'in, at, on, etc'. On the other hand, *dyáryo* [ʤá:ryo] 'newspaper' is one of the borrowed words from Spanish. It seems that *tiyán~tyán* [tʃá(.)n] 'belly' is a native word, while *tsá* [tʃá] 'tea' and *intsík* ['intʃík] 'Chinese' are borrowed words. [tʃ] is also analyzed as the sequence of /t/ and /s/, because Tagalog has no word that includes [ts]. [ʃ] appears in the environment /siyV.../ (V symbolizes vowels). This is phonemicized as /siyV.../.

#### 2.3.4. Syllable structure

It is evident that the syllable structure of Tagalog is basically (C)V(C), and the words consist of (C)V(C) + ((C)V(C)) ..., which is formally represented by $\{(C)V(C)\}_1$. By the subscript $_1$ is meant that words consist of at least one (C)V(C). Note that the syllable structure formalized above does not apply to words such as *trabaho* 'job', *intsik* 'Chinese', etc. Thus, the structure $\{(C(C))V(C)\}_1$ is a more comprehensive formula for words in Tagalog, including *trabaho* 'job' and *intsik* 'Chinese' that are not native to Tagalog. The syllable structure of words like *araw* 'sun, day' and *trabaho* 'job' are V/CVC and CCV/CV/CV, respectively, where the symbol / represents syllable boundary.

## 2.4. Prosody

Stress plays a critical role in distinguishing word meanings, while length does or does not accompany it, depending on phonological environments. Thus, stress has phonemic status, represented by /´/. See the following examples.

(16) a. hápon [há:pon] 'afternoon', Hapón [hapó(.)n] 'Japanese'
  b. bába' [bá:ba'] 'chin', babá' [babá'] 'descent',
  c. búkas [bú:kas] 'tomorrow', bukás [buká(.)s] 'open'
  d. sáya [sá:ya] 'long skirt', sayá [sayá] 'happiness'

As is clear from the examples above, the appearance of length is predictable. In word-final syllables, whether open or closed, length does not appear, e.g. *manók* 'chicken', *ulán* 'rain', *totoó* 'true', *anó* 'what', etc. When the word-final consonants are sonorant, however, the stressed vowels preceding them may be somewhat prolonged, which can be represented by [.]. Except in word-final syllables, the stressed vowel in open syllables is prolonged as can be notated by [:]. In conclusion, [:] and [.] are not given phonemic status.

## 2.5. Borrowed words

What I have described so far makes it clear which words are borrowed. To give examples, words that include /e/ and /o/ in non-final syllables, words that begin with or end in /r/, and words in which word-final vowels are long, e.g. jeepney [ʤí:pni:]. In addition, there are a lot of borrowed words that cannot be distinguished from native words, because they match the phonological pattern of native words: e.g. *asúkal* 'sugar' (Spanish), *mukhá'* 'face' (Sanskrit), *papél* 'paper' (Spanish), etc.

## 2.6. Stress rules

Verbs in Tagalog inflect for aspect, represented by the symbols *PF*, *IMPF*, etc. The root word (RW) of verbs usually consists of two syllables, which can be divided into two types. One is the type whose stress is laid on the first or initial syllable and the other is the type whose stress is on the second or final syllable.

Example (17) represents the *-um-* verbs and their inflections and example (18) the *mag-* verbs and their inflections. Clearly, we can predict where the stress is placed on inflectional forms. Thus, it suffices to mark where the stress is placed on the RW.

(17) *-um-* verbs and their inflections
   a. puntá 'to go': p-um-untá (NT/IMP, PF), p-um-ú-puntá (IMPF), pú-puntá (INCP)
   b. káin 'to eat': k-um-áin (NT/IMP, PF), k-um-a-káin (IMPF), ka-káin (INCP)

(18) *mag-* verbs and their inflections
   a. laró 'to play': mag-laró (NT/IMP), nag-laró (PF), nag-lá-laró (IMPF), mag-lá-laró (INCP)
   b. áral 'to study': mag-áral (NT/IMP), nag-áral (PF), nag-a-áral (IMPF), mag-a-áral (INCP)

To conclude, the following rules effectively predict where the stress appears in verb inflections. Note that the morphological information on reduplication (RED) makes the stress rules simple.

(19) a. $S_2\acute{S}_1\# \to (\text{RÉD})S_2\acute{S}_1\#$, where RÉD involves the first (C)V of RWs.
   b. $\acute{S}_2 S_1\# \to$ Vacant

Finally, a word must be said about stress shift. The suffixes *-hin* and *-han* shift the stress one syllable to the right, as seen below.

(20) a. inóm 'to drink': inum-ín (NT/IMP), in-inóm (PF), in-í-inóm (IMPF), í-inum-ín (INCP)

b. bása 'to read': basá-hin (NT/IMP), b-in-ása (PF), b-in-a-bása (IMPF), bá-basá-hin (INCP)

Examples (20a) and (20b) can be described in terms of the following stress rules:

(21) a. $S_2\acute{S}_1$ + (h)in# → (RÉD)$S_2S_1$ + (h)ín# : (NT/IMP, INCP)
$S_2\acute{S}_1$# → (RÉD)$S_2\acute{S}_1$# : (PF, IMPF)
b. $\acute{S}_2S_1$ + (h)in# → (RÉD)$S_2\acute{S}_1$ + (h)in# : (NT/IMP, INCP)
$\acute{S}_2S_1$ → Vacant: (IMPF, PF)

# Part I

# Words and Sentences

# Chapter 3
# Typological characteristics of Tagalog

## 3.1. Introduction

It is well known that Tagalog is a verb-initial language. Furthermore, the voice system is unique in that more than two voices are found. Thus, it is more plausible to call this type of voice system the **multi-voiced system** than to use the term **focus-system** that has been widely used in Philippine linguistics. What is more, the question remains open as to whether Tagalog is morphologically ergative or accusative, which has long attracted our attention typologically. An attempt will be made in this chapter to examine the typological characteristics of Tagalog in depth.

## 3.2. Verb-initial language

When a sentence consists of Subject (S), Object (O) and Verb (V), the following word orders are logically possible.

( 1 ) SOV, SVO, VSO, VOS, OSV, OVS

In relation to (1), two points must be taken into account. First, which NP can be identified as S(UBJ)? By and large, the NP that corresponds to Agent tends to be identified as S. This is the case with accusative languages. The opposite is true, however, of ergative languages. To take an example from Dyirbal, an Australian language, the Patient NP is treated as S. Thus, it must be necessary to make clear what properties accompany the subject NP. Second, the six combinations in (1) are unevenly distributed across the world's languages, as shown in (2) (cf. also Steel 1978). It seems that the frequency of the six combinations has to do with our ability to process information.

( 2 ) a. SOV=45%, b. SVO=35%, c. VSO=18%, d. VOS=2%, e. OSV=0%,
f. OVS=0%

Peripherally, there is a language that manifests OVS: Hixkaryana, a language of the Amazon Basin. Note that the frequency in (2) is based on the word order of *unmarked* constructions. In the marked constructions, however, languages allow some variation. In Japanese, a typical SOV language, sentences with OSV appear, as in *Sono hon boku yon-da yo* (the book I read-PAST FP) 'The book I read (it)'.

Let us now consider why Tagalog is allowed to begin with V, despite the fact that about 80 % of the world's languages begin with S. It is assumed that the SOV or SVO order is unmarked, which implies that in expressing an idea, we present an entity first and then talk about it. Conversely, when a verb begins a sentence, the verb itself conveys information equivalent to the sentence as a whole (cf. also Nichols 1986: 56-119).

We are in a good position to examine what information must be encoded in an initial verb. To put it another way, what is crucial for the verb in a verb-initial language? The answer is that the initial verb must convey information equivalent to the sentence as a whole or information equivalent to SOV or SVO as a whole. Thus, the verb must encode the information on the semantic role of the subject (and the object), voice, tense/aspect, etc. The following subsections aim to clarify how the initial verb marks the information overtly.

### 3.2.1. Voice

Let us take an example from English in order to examine the voice phenomenon. English has two voices, i.e. active and passive. Observe the following pair of sentences.

( 3 ) a. John kissed Jane.
    b. Jane was kissed by John.

Clearly, sentences (3a) and (3b) have the same conceptual meaning. Their difference lies in which NP is the subject. Thus, the voice phenomenon can be defined as a relationship between the subject and the verb (cf. Shibatani 1997, 1998). It must be noted here that the grammatical relation *object* is not relevant to the definition of voice. This implies that an intransitive sentence has to do with the voice phenomenon. The following are examples from Tagalog.

( 4 ) a. P-um-unta     ako         kay Jane sa Kobe.
       Ci-AV.FN-go  1SG.NOM  to   Jane in  Kobe
       'I went to Jane in Kobe.'
    b. P-in-unta-han     ko              si   Jane sa Kobe.
       Ci-FN-go-DIR  1SG.ng-A.  SM Jane in  Kobe.
       'I went to Jane in Kobe.'

(4a) is an intransitive sentence whose subject is *ako* 'I'. In (4b), on the other hand, *Jane* is the subject. (4a) and (4b) have the same conceptual meaning. Thus, (4b) can be regarded as an alternative to (4a). (4a) is Agent-voiced (AV), while (4b) is Directional/Locative-voiced (DV). By the same token, Palauan, an Austronesian language of Micronesia, has this type of voice variation, as seen below (Foley and Van Valin 1985: 316-7).

(5) a.  A     ngelek-ek  a   s[m]e'er          er    a    tereter.
        ART   child-my       [INTRANS]-sick  with  ART  cold
        'My child is sick with a cold.'
    b.  A     tereter   a    l-se'er      er    ngiy  a    ngelek-ek.
        ART   cold           PASS 3SG-sick with  3SG  ART  child-my
        'With a cold is being sick by my child.'
        [ART: article, INTRANS: intransitive verb, PASS: passive, SG: singular, 3: third person]

(5b) is an example in which the Causal NP is the subject. Incidentally, German has passives of intransitive sentences with *es* 'it' as the subject: *Es wurde gestern getanzt* (it became yesterday danced: 'There was dancing yesterday' (Keenan 1985: 274)).

In relation to the voice phenomenon, a word must be said about *markedness*. Markedness plays an important role in defining the voice phenomenon. As is clear from (3), the passive in English is marked by **be** + *(V)-en* on the verb, while the active counterpart has just *V*. Thus, it can be assumed that the passive is marked and the active is unmarked. This contrast is characteristic of languages that show the active/passive dichotomy. Note, however, that the active/passive dichotomy is not found in Tagalog. Nevertheless. Bloomfield (1917), Wolff (1973), Constantino (2000) and others classify Tagalog as a language whose voice system is dichotomous. Wolff's (1973) classification, for instance, is problematic in that it classifies passives into three categories (see Table 3–1).

Table 3–1: Classification of voices (Wolff 1973: 72)

| Voices | Active  |                      |
|--------|---------|----------------------|
|        | Passive | Local passive        |
|        |         | Direct passive       |
|        |         | Instrumental passive |

Let us now turn to how verbs in Tagalog are marked for voice. Tagalog has voice variations like (6) below, adapted from Campbell (1995: 515). (6) illustrates that the various sentences occur depending on which NP is chosen as the subject from candidate NPs or Adverbial Phrases, where the subject NP is marked with *ang* (common nouns) or *si* (human proper nouns). The *ng*-marked patient (*ng* : [naŋ]) indicates an indefinite reference, while the *ang*-marked patient a definite reference.

(6) a. AV: B-um-i-bilí    si    Pédro ng    aklát sa báyan pára kay Fidél.
    C$_i$-AV-UF-buy SM Pedro ng-P book in town    for    Fidel
    'Pedro always buys books in the town for Fidel.'

b. PV: B-in-i-bilí    ni    Pédro ang aklát sa báyan
    Ci-PV.BG-UF-buy PN.SG.ng-A Pedro SM book in town
    pára kay Fidél.
    for    Fidel
    'Pedro buys the book in the town for Fidel.'

c. LV: B-in-i-bil-hán    ni    Pédro ng aklát ang báyan
    Ci-BG-UF-buy-LV PN.SG.ng-A Pedro ng-P book SM town
    pára kay Fidél.
    for    Fidel
    'The town is the place where Pedro buys books for Fidel.'

d. BV: I-b-in-i-bilí    ni    Pédro ng aklát sa báyan
    BV-Ci-BG-UF-buy PN.SG.ng-A Pedro ng-P book in town

si                    Fidél.
PN.SG.NOM    Fidel
'Fidel is being bought a book by Pedro in the town.'

Note that when the subject plays an Agent role like *Pedro* in (6a), the infix *-um-* is inserted before the first vowel of the verb stem *bili* 'to buy' (i.e. root word), producing *b-um-ili*. This relationship between the verb *b-um-ili* and the subject *Pedro* (Agent) is in the agent-voice (AV). Although this relationship seems similar to the active voice in English, the active voice and the agent voice are different in that the former is not marked, but the latter is marked by *-um-*. In addition, the sentences in (6) manifest subjects with different semantic roles, while the active/passive dichotomy manifests subjects with two roles, i.e. agent and patient. See Table 3–2, for the voice system in Tagalog.

Table 3–2: Voice system in Tagalog

| Voice | Subject NP | Marking |
| --- | --- | --- |
| Agent Voice (AV) | si Pedro | -um- |
| Patient Voice (PV) | ang aklat 'book' | -in-/-hin |
| Locative Voice (LV) | ang bayan 'town' | -han |
| Benefactive Voice (BV) | si Fidel | i- |

As is clear from the discussion so far, Tagalog shows **voice variation**, which is in marked contrast to the bipartition between the active and the passive, where the active is not marked and the passive is marked.

We are now in a better position to explain voice variation in Tagalog, focusing on verb marking. It is important to note that each voice form in Tagalog must be marked, with the result that the AV form is not so frequently used as the active voice in English, which has to do with the fact that when the Patient NP is definite, a patient-voiced (PV) form automatically surfaces, since the *ng*-marked

Patient NP represents an indefinite reference, as mentioned above. In conclusion, the voice variation in Tagalog produces the voice system with more than two voices, which is now termed **multi-voiced**.

The multi-voiced type of language can be described in terms of a framework within which the underlying structure (US) is posited. The US is not marked for voice, which is represented by the neutral voice (NV). The US conveys information on a verb and its arguments, from which actual sentences are formed. This can be schematized in (7).

(7) US          Voice Alternations

| NV | → | AV | PV | LV/DV | BV | IV | Others |

This framework properly describes how actual sentences surface and makes clear why each voice in Tagalog is marked.

### 3.2.2. Tense and aspect

Verbal root words (RW, see Chapter 7) in Tagalog are marked for aspects. See Table 3–3 below.

Table 3–3: Aspects in Tagalog

| Aspects | *bili* 'to buy' | *alis* 'to leave' | *luto* 'to cook' | Gloss |
|---|---|---|---|---|
| Neutral | b-um-ili | um-alis | mag-luto' | (Ci-)AV.NT-RW |
| Imperative | b-um-ili | um-alis | mag-luto' | (Ci-)AV.IMP-RW |
| Perfective | b-um-ili | um-alis | nag-luto' | (Ci-)AV.FN-RW |
| Imperfective | b-um-i-bili | um-a-alis | nag-lu-luto' | (Ci-)AV-UF-RW |
| Inceptive | bi-bili | a-alis | mag-lu-luto' | AV.(-)NB-RW |

Aspects denote whether the event or action at issue has finished, is still in the process, or will take place (in the near future), without reference to the time of utterance. The sentences in (8) below are examples in which aspects play a central role in Tagalog. See the verb inflections and the translation equivalents.

(8) a. Nag-lu-lúto'   ng     pagkáin ang nánay   noóng d-um-atíng
       AV-UF-cook ng-P food    SM mother when  $C_i$-AF.FN-arrive
       akó.
       1SG.NOM
       'Mother was cooking some food when I arrived.'
       (Schachter and Otanes 1972: 67)
   b. Nang nag-ta-trabáho siyá sa pábrika, malakí ang suwéldo niyá.
      when AV-UF-work s/he in factory big SM pay his/her
      'When he was working at the factory, his pay was large.'
      (Schachter and Otanes 1972: 476)
   c. Nang  a-alís        na      akó,     t-in-áwag      niyá
      when AV.NB-leave already 1SG.NOM $C_i$-PV.FN-call 3SG.ng-A
      akó.
      1SG.NOM
      'When I was about to leave, he called me.'
      (Schachter and Otanes 1972: 477)

Note that in the sentences above, the imperfective forms are used even when the action refers to the past, where in English the past progressive forms must be used. Incidentally, Himmelmann (2005: 363) divides aspects further into Realis and Non-realis.

### 3.2.3. How to gloss the aspects

In the examples in (6) and (8) above, I used abbreviations like UF and BG to mark aspects on the verbs. Now we need to explain what these abbreviations mean.

(9) a. Neutral: **NT**
　　b. Imperative: **IMP**
　　c. Perfective: **FN** (finished)
　　d. Imperfective: (**BG**: begun), **UF** (unfinished)
　　e. Inceptive: **NB** (not begun)

The imperfective can be represented by UF only. This is because BG is redundant, although BG is used in the examples in (6) to show explicitly the correspondence between the form and the gloss.

It is to be noted that reduplications are frequently used. Roughly speaking, reduplication indicates that the action at issue has not finished yet. Thus, it turns out that reduplications appear in the imperfective and inceptive forms. The first syllable ((C)V) of RWs is repeated in reduplication.

## 3.3. Is Tagalog morphologically ergative or accusative?

Before discussing the ergative/accusative controversy in Tagalog, it is necessary to take a brief look at the notions of morphological ergativity and accusativity.

When sentences consist of S, A and P, to the exclusion of V, ergative languages treat S and P alike, where S and P are termed absolutive and A is termed ergative. Accusative languages, on the other hand, treat S and A alike, when S and A are termed nominative and P is termed accusative.

It has often been assumed that Tagalog is an ergative language (e.g. Payne 1982, Nolasco 2005, etc.). In contrast, I argue that Tagalog is neither ergative nor accusative, but **multi-voiced.** After looking at non-ergative properties of Tagalog, Foley (2008) provides the term *symmetrical* for this type of language. In the following, we shall look at the ergative and accusative properties of Tagalog.

Observe the following pair of sentences, which manifest accusative morphology. See Table 3–4.

(10) a. P-um-u-puntá *ang* mga báta' sa eskuwelahán.
                                            (*mga* is pronounced [maŋa])
      $C_i$-AV-UF-go  SM(NOM)  PL  child to  school
      'The students go to school.'
   b. B-um-a-bása   ***ng***   mga libró *ang*   mga báta'.
      $C_i$-AV-UF-read  ACC  PL  book  SM(NOM)  PL  child
      'The children are reading books.'

Table 3–4: Accusative morphology

| V | S<br>*ang* |          |
|---|------------|----------|
| V | A<br>*ang* | **P**<br>***ng*** |

Let us now compare (11a) and (11b), which show ergative morphology. See Table 3–5 below.

(11) a. T-um-akbó   *ang*  báta'.
      Ci-AV.FN-run  ABS  child
      'The child ran.'
   b. B-in-ása     ***ng***   mga báta' *ang* mga libró.
      Ci-PV.FN-read  ERG  PL  child  ABS  PL  book
      'The children read the books.'

Table 3–5: Ergative morphology

| V | S<br>*ang*        |                |
|---|-------------------|----------------|
| V | **A**<br>***ng*** | P<br>*ang*     |

It is clear from Tables 3–4 and 3–5 that Tagalog has both ergative and accusative properties, which can be related to syntactic processes through which subject is identified (Schachter 1976, 1977). It seems that these properties have much to do with the multi-voiced character of Tagalog. By and large, Tagalog cannot be classified into either accusative or ergative. Rather, it is a multi-voiced language.

Now the distribution of case markers in Tagalog can be captured in the following table.

Table 3–6: Case distributions

| Voices | Agent NP | Patient NP | Other NP |
|---|---|---|---|
| AV | ang NP/si PN | ng NP/*ni PN | sa NP/kay PN |
| PV | ng NP/ni PN | ang NP/si PN | sa NP/kay PN |
| Non-AV/PV | ng NP/ni PN | ng NP/*ni PN | ang NP/si PN |

Why *ng-A* and *ng-P* are used instead of terms such as genitive and accusative is to stay on neutral ground in the accusative and the ergative analysis. In terms of the ergative analysis, *ng-A* can readily be treated as the ergative case, when *ang-NP* is the absolutive case. In the accusative treatment, *ng-A* and *ng-P* mark the genitive case and the accusative case, respectively, where *ng-P* cannot be termed genitive, because *ng-A* and *ng-P* are different; *ng-A* denotes a definite/indefinite reference, while *ng-P* an indefinite reference.

In the sequence of N1 + N2 (N1: possessed, N2: possessor), N2 is in the genitive case whose reference is [±definite]. N2 consists of *ng NP* or *ni PN*.

Thus, the distinction between *ng-A* and *ng-P* is useful in justifying that Tagalog is neither ergative nor accusative. As mentioned before, Tagalog can be best understood as a multi-voiced language.

# Chapter 4

# Sentence types

## 4.1. Unmarked and marked constructions

Two types of construction can be distinguished in Tagalog. That is, unmarked and marked constructions. The difference between them lies in whether topicalization can be applied or not. Unmarked constructions can be topicalized, where the topic marker *ay* is inserted. They are autonomous as a clause. Marked constructions, on the other hand, cannot be topicalized, because they are not autonomous as a clause. For more information on topicalization, see Chapter 17.

Table 4–1: Classification of Tagalog sentences

| Markedness | Sentence types |
|---|---|
| Unmarked constructions | a. Situational<br>b. Indefinite<br>c. Definite<br>d. Possessive<br>e. Others |
| Marked constructions | a. Noun + Clause type<br>b. Gusto – construction<br>c. Existential<br>d. Subjectless<br>e. Others |

For the classification based on topicalization, see Table 4–1 above.

## 4.2. Unmarked constructions

In this section, we shall deal with unmarked constructions. In §.4.2.1 and §.4.2.2, we focus on the types of sentence that Constantino (1970, 1971, 2000) has proposed: situational, indefinite and definite sentences.

### 4.2.1. Situational sentences

Tagalog **basic** sentences can be classified into the following types (Constantino 1970, 1971, 2000).

( 1 ) Types of basic sentence in Tagalog
    a. Situational sentence
    b. Indefinite sentence
    c. Definite sentence

Let us first look at type (1a), i.e. situational sentences. Situational sentences consist of Predicate + Subject, now reformulated as $IC_1 + IC_2$. The predicate involves at least one of the following phrases: Verb Phrases (VP), Adjective Phrases (AP), Noun Phrases (NP) and Prepositional Phrases (PP). See the following examples, where VP, AP, NP and PP appear in this order.

( 2 ) a. T-um-akbó     ang báta'. (VP)
      Ci-AV.FN-run   SM child
      'The child ran.'
   b. Magandá-ng magandá ang babáe-ng itó. (AP)
      beautiful-LK beautiful   SM girl-LK   this
      'This girl is very beautiful.'

(NB: The linker serves to connect a modifier and a modifiee. It is also used to connect a relative clause with its head. For more information on the linker, see Chapter 8.)

c. Estudyánte siyá. (NP)
   student    3SG.NOM
   'S/he is a student.'

d. Nása báhay si   Nóri. (PP)
   in   house SM Nori
   'Nori is at home.'

In situational sentences, the subject NP has the following properties: it is preceded by the subject marker or the nominative case marker *ang* (with common nouns), or *si/sina* (with human proper nouns), it occurs in IC2 position, and its semantic role is marked by the verbal affixes. In (2a), for example, the infix *-um-* indicates that the subject is the Agent NP *báta'* 'child'. It is important to note that this is a sort of subject-verb agreement, although it differs from that in European languages, since the subject-verb agreement in European languages involves verbs that inflect for person, number, etc. Thus, the particle *ang* in Tagalog serves as the 'subject marker' rather than the 'topic marker', despite the fact that the term 'topic marker' has long been used in Philippine linguistics (Hirano 2005).

We shall now turn to the situational sentences that have Patient NPs.

(3) a. B-um-a-bása     ng    libró/aklát ang estudyánte.
       $C_i$-AV-UF-read ng-P book        SM  student
       'The student is reading a book.'

    b. B-um-a-bása     siyá    ng    libró.
       $C_i$-AV-UF-read 3SG.NOM ng-P book
       'S/he is reading a book.'

The examples above show that the AV situational sentences have VOS or VSO order. When the subject is a personal pronoun, VSO order appears. When the subject is a common noun, VOS order is preferred.

The situational sentences dealt with so far can be formalized as follows:

Table 4–2: Formulation of situational sentences

| Verb or Predicate types | NP | NP |
| --- | --- | --- |
| ITRV | | ang NP (S) |
| NP/AP/PP | | ang NP (S) |
| TRV | ng NP (O) | ang NP (S) |
| TRV | PRN (S) | ng NP (O) |

## 4.2.2. Indefinite and definite sentences

In this section, we shall illustrate indefinite and definite sentences with examples. As will be seen below, their difference lies in the form of $IC_1$. In indefinite sentences, $IC_1$ is not headed by *ang*, while in definite sentences, it is headed by *ang*.

(4) a. Indefinite sentence
　　　Báta' ang t-um-akbó.
　　　child SM Ci-AV.FN-run
　　　'It is a child who ran.'
　　b. Definite sentence
　　　Ang báta' ang t-um-akbó.
　　　DET child SM Ci-AV.FN-run
　　　'It is the child who ran.'

For the different treatment of *ang* in (4b), see Chapter 5.

Now the three types of sentence can be summarized in Table 4–3.

Table 4–3: Types of basic sentences

| Types | IC1: Predicate | IC2: Subject | Meaning |
|---|---|---|---|
| Situational | T-um-akbó<br>Ci-AV.FN-run | ang  bátaʼ<br>SM    child | The child ran. |
| Indefinite | Bátaʼ<br>child | ang  t-um-akbó<br>SM    Ci-AV.FN-run | It is a child who ran. |
| Definite | Ang    báta<br>DET    child | ang  t-um-akbó<br>SM    Ci-AV.FN-run | It is the child who ran. |

Table 4–3 shows that the particle *ang* in IC$_2$ position serves to form a headless relative clause, which implies that the particles *ang*, *ng* [naŋ] and *sa* have the nominalization function, along with the case marking function. Reid (2002) suggests that the particle *ang* serves as a definite marker.

It is important to note that the Tagalog equivalent of *who ran?* is not (5) below, which is in marked contrast to the formation of *wh*-questions in English. *Wh*-questions in Tagalog are formed by the structure in which the particle *ang* immediately precedes IC$_2$, as shown in (6). Thus, *wh*-questions in Tagalog look like cleft sentences.

( 5 ) *Síno tumakbó?
    who  ran
    Intended: 'Who ran?'

( 6 ) Síno ang  tumakbó?
    who  SM   ran
    'Who ran?'

## 4.2.3. Possessives

Possessives and existentials have something in common, because both of them use the verb form *may*. The difference between them lies in that possessives have a subject NP, while existentials do not. Instead, adverbs of place are required for existentials. Thus, existentials are categorized as subjectless sentences. See the following examples.

( 7 ) a. May    marámi-ng libró  ang estudyánte.    (**Possessive**)
have/exist many-LK  book SM student
'The student has a lot of books.'
b. May    marámi-ng libró  sa aklátan.    (**Existential**)
have/exist many-LK  book in library
'There are plenty of books in the library.'

( 8 ) a. Ang estudyánte ay    may    marámi-ng libró.  (**Topicalization**)
SM student    TM have/exist many-LK  book
'The student has a lot of books.'
b. ??Sa aklátan ay    may    marámi-ng libró.  (**Topicalization**)
in library    TM have/exist many-LK  book
'There are plenty of books in the library.'

(8b) may be possible. This is an example of adjunct topicalization (cf. Hirano 2010).

## 4.3. Marked constructions

As mentioned in Section 4.1, topicalization cannot apply to marked constructions. This has to do with the fact that marked constructions do not have clausal status. In what follows, we shall take a brief look at marked constructions.

### 4.3.1. Noun + Clause type

The Noun + Clause type is unique in that it begins with a noun, where the initial nouns are restricted to *mukhá* 'face', *pára* 'apparent, seeming', *tíla* 'it seems', etc. It is true that the question remains of whether they are nouns, adjectives or adverbs. In fact, English (1986) defines *pára* and *tíla* as adverbs. Interestingly enough, *mukhá* 'face' is of Sanskrit origin. *Pára* is also a borrowed word from Spanish. It may be assumed that the *mukhá* construction was formed by the influence of the *parece que* construction in Spanish, which is equivalent to *(it) seems that* in English. See (9a), an example where *mukhá* is used. (9b) is the formalization of this type.

(9) a. Mukhá-ng  u-ulán.                    (English 1986: 916)
       face-LK    AV.NB-rain
       'It seems that it will rain.'
    b. [N + CLAUSE]

The LK (linker) in (9a) serves as the complementizer [COMP]. For more information on various functions of linker, see Chapter 8. Incidentally, *u-ulán* is a subjectless sentence with the meaning 'it will rain'.

### 4.3.2. Gusto-construction

The *Gusto*-construction is similar to the N + Clause type, because *gusto* is originally a noun with the meaning 'preference' (see English 1986: 554). *Gustó* forms the following types of construction.

(10) a. Gustó ko        **ng**     manggá.      (NB: *ng* is pronounced [naŋ].)
        like  1SG.ng-A  ng-P       mango
        'I want **a** mango.'
     b. Gustó ko        **ang**    manggá.
        like  1SG.ng-A  NOM        mango
        'I want **the** mango.'

    c. Gustó ko-ng         k-um-ain    ng    manggá.
                                                         (NB: -*ng* is pronounced [ŋ].)
       like   1SG.ng-A-LK  Ci-AV.NT    ng-P  mango
       'I want to eat a mango.'

Note that in (10b), I glossed *ang* as NOM. For the use and function of *ang*, see Chapter 5. Examples (10a) and (10b) are similar to what is called the non-canonical constructions in Japanese. The non-canonical constructions in Japanese are transitive sentences with the *ni*-marked subject and the *ga*-marked object, or with the *ga*-marked subject and the *ga*-marked object. (10a) and (10b) are non-canonical, because they consist of the genitive subject and the accusative or nominative object, to follow the accusative analysis. It is important to note that (10c) resembles the Noun + Clause type. The *Gusto*-construction can be formalized as follows:

(11) a. [N-ng-A/GEN + N]   (10a, 10b)
     b. [N-ng-A/GEN + CLAUSE]   (10c)

Alternatively, *gustó* can be treated as an Auxiliary-like verb. Note that *gustó* is a borrowed word from Spanish. The native counterpart of this is *íbig* 'love, fondness, affection' (English 1986: 676).

Other auxiliary-like verbs like *kailángan* 'necessary' and *dápat* 'must' are similar to the *gusto* type in structure. For 'Auxiliary-like verbs', see Chapter 23. Incidentally, the *Gusto*-construction may be relatable to the N + Clause type. In relation to this, see the schemata (9b) and (11b).

### 4.3.3. Existential

The difference between existentials and possessives has been described in Section 4.2.3. In this section, therefore, I will illustrate further examples of existentials.

See the following sentences.

(12) a. May       marámi-ng péra    sa bángko.
     have/exist much-LK   money in bank
     'There is much money in the bank.'
   b. May       limá-ng báta' sa báhay niyá.
     have/exist five-LK child in house 3SG.GEN
     'There are five children in his/her house.'

### 4.3.4. Subjectless sentences

In English, the empty subject *it* is used to describe meteorology, temperature, etc. The Tagalog equivalents of the constructions are expressed by subjectless sentences, because it has no dummy subject. Additionally, it is clear that the absence of the dummy *it* makes extraposition impossible. Illustrative sentences may serve to make the point much clearer. See the following examples.

(13) a. Um-ulán        kahápon.
       AV.FN-rain yesterday
       'It rained yesterday.'                          (**Meteorology**)
   b. Maliwánag sa kuwárto  námin.
       bright      in room   1PL.EXCL.GEN
       'It is bright in our room.'                   (**Darkness/brightness**)
   c. L-um-indól           kahápon.          (English 1986: 117)
       Ci-AV.FN-earthquake yesterday
       'There was an earthquake yesterday.'     (**Natural phenomenon**)
   d. Ka-ra-ratíng      lang ni     Tóny gáling sa kláse.
       RF-RED-arrive just PN.SG.ng-A Tony from    class
       'Tony has just arrived from class.'          (**Recently finished**)

e. Anó-ng gandá ni Tína!
   what-LK beauty PN.SG.GEN/ng-A Tina
   'What a beautiful lady Tina is!' (**Exclamation**)
f. Kay gandá ni Tína!
   EXC beauty PN.SG.GEN/ng-A Tina
   'How beautiful Tina is!' (**Exclamation**)

# Chapter 5

# The particle *ang*

In the preceding chapter, we dealt with sentence types, where the particle *ang* was glossed as SM (subject marker) or DET (determiner). In this chapter, we examine the particle *ang* in more detail, focusing on the function of the particle *ang* that appears in IC$_2$ position. I will show here that the particle *ang* in IC$_2$ position serves to mark subject. Thus, I gloss the particle *ang* as SM (subject marker). This assumption is in sharp contrast to the practice of Philippine linguistics, where the particle *ang* has long been termed TM (topic marker).

We shall now illustrate phrases and sentences in which the particle *ang* is used.

( 1 ) *ang*-phrases
    a. ang libró
       the book
       'the book'
    b. ang libró-ng  s-in-úlat       ni       Nóri
       the book-LK  Ci-PV.FN-write  PN.SG.ng-A  Nori
       'the book that was written by Nori' or 'the book that Nori wrote'

  c. ang táo-ng s-um-úlat  ng libró
   the man-LK Ci-AV.FN-write ng-P book
   'the man who wrote a book'
  d. ang s-um-úlat  ng libró
   the Ci-AV.FN-write ng-P book
   'the one who wrote a book'
   (The function of LK will be detailed in Chapter 8.)

( 2 ) *ang*-sentences (cf. Constantino 1970, 1971, 2000)
  a. T-um-akbó  ang báta'.
   Ci-AV.FN-run SM child
   'The child ran.'
  b. Báta' ang t-um-akbó.
   child SM Ci-AV.FN-run
   'It is a child who ran.'
  c. Ang báta' ang t-um-akbó.
   DET child SM Ci-AV.FN-run
   'It is the child who ran.'

Note that (2a) covers situational sentences that consist of AP/NP/VP and NP.

  In describing a language, a distinction must be made between grammatical relations and case markers. As mentioned above, we glossed the particle *ang* as subject marker (SM) or determiner (DET). However, there arises a serious question when we gloss *ang* as determiner, since the determiner is neither a case marker nor a grammatical relation. How do we treat these two functions (i.e. SM and DET) of *ang* neatly? All in all, we conclude that the particle *ang* in $IC_2$ position denotes the subject, which is definite and in the nominative case, while the particle *ang* in $IC_1$ position and in forms that do not constitute a sentence serves as the determiner (DET).

The particle *ang* in IC$_1$ and that in IC$_2$ are, in a sense, in complementary distribution. The former is the determiner, while the latter is the subject marker. Thus, in (2a) above, the particle *ang* serves as the subject marker. In (2b), it is the subject marker that forms a headless relative clause through nominalization. This distribution implies that the particle *ang* once served as a determiner and it has been grammaticalized into the subject marker (see Shibatani 1991).

We are now in a position to explain how the particle *ang* is glossed.

(3) *ang*-phrases
    a. ang    libró
       DET  book
    b. ang    libró-ng    b-in-asa         ni          Nóri
       DET  book-LK  Ci-PV.FN-read  PN.SG.ng-A  Nori
    c. ang    táo-ng    s-um-úlat        ng    libró
       DET  man-LK  Ci-AV.FN-write  ng-P  book
    d. ang    s-um-úlat        ng    libró
       DET  Ci-AV.FN-write  ng-P  book

(4) *ang*-sentences
    a. T-um-akbó      ang  báta'.
       Ci-AV.FN-run  SM  child
    b. Báta' ang t-um-akbó.
       child  SM  Ci-AV.FN-run
    c. Ang  báta'  ang  t-um-akbó.
       DET  child  SM  Ci-AV.FN-run

The particle *ang* and *si* have the same function. Their difference lies in the fact that *ang* precedes a common noun, while *si* a human proper noun. Thus, *si* can be glossed as SM.

Finally, a word must be said about the nominalization function of *ang* as in (3d). This *ang* serves to form a headless relative clause or a nominalization with a definite reference. Case particles such as *ng* [naŋ] and *sa* also serve to form a headless relative clause or a nominalization, as shown below.

(5) Nag-bigáy akó ng mga kéndi sa b-um-a-bása ng libró.
AV.FN-give 1SG.NOM ng-P PL candy to Ci-AV-UF-read ng-P book
'I gave candies to the one who was reading a book.'
(NB: *mga* is pronounced [maŋá].)

(6) Ang áming báhay ay naka-tayó' sa may simbáhan.
(English 1986: 1397)
SM 1PL.EXCL.LK house TM STAT-stand in/at exist church
'Our house is situated by the church.'

Note that in (6), *sa may simbáhan* means 'in the place where a church is located'.

For the subject status of the particle *ang*, see also Adams and Manaster-Ramer (1998).

## Chapter 6

## Nouns and verbs in Tagalog

Himmelman (2005: 361), Gil (1993) and others argue that Tagalog does not make a distinction between nouns and verbs. Specifically, they assume that there is no clear-cut distinction among contents words in Tagalog. In this chapter, we argue that Tagalog formally distinguishes between nouns and verbs. Incidentally, Smith (2009) makes it clear that phonologically every language makes a distinction between nouns and verbs.

Before continuing, let us observe the examples that Gil (1993: 394) cites. Based on these examples, he assumes that Tagalog does not distinguish nouns from verbs. Glosses in (1) are mine. English translations are Gil's.

( 1 ) a. Pulubi ang bangkero.
    beggar SM boatman
    'The boatman is a beggar.'
  b. Pulubi ang b-um-alik.
    beggar SM Ci-AV.FN-return
    'The one who returned is a beggar.'

c. Pulubi ang mabait.
   beggar SM kind
   'The kind one is a beggar.'
d. P-in-atay ang bangkero.
   Ci-PV.FN-kill SM boatman
   'The boatman was killed.'
e. P-in-atay ang b-um-alik.
   Ci-PV.FN-kill SM Ci-AV.FN-return
   'The one who returned was killed.'
f. P-in-atay ang mabait.
   Ci-PV.FN-kill SM kind
   'The kind one was killed.'
g. Mapayat ang bangkero.
   thin SM boatman
   'The boatman is thin.'
h. Mapayat ang b-um-alik.
   thin SM Ci-AV.FN-return
   'The one who returned is thin.'
i. Mapayat ang mabait.
   thin SM kind
   'The kind one is thin.'

Gil's assumption presupposes that what corresponds to English nouns, verbs and adjectives can occur before and after the particle *ang*. Attention must be paid, however, to the fact that the particle *ang* can appear before nouns, verbs and adjectives, rather than the presupposition that *pulubi*, *bangkero*, *bumalik*, *mabait* and *mapayat* can appear before and after the particle *ang*. When *ang* appears before a noun, it serves as the determiner. When it appears before a verb or an adjective, it serves as a nominalizer. Needless to say, both types of *ang* function as subject marker when it appears in IC2 position. Thus, it can be said that *N*, *V* and *ADJ* in Tagalog are all able to have a noun-like function when they are preceded by the particle *ang*. This description of *ang* justifies the fact that the following are also grammatical, although they are not given in (1).

(2) a. Mapayat ang p-in-atay.
     thin     SM Ci-PV.FN-kill
     'The one who was killed was thin.'
  b. Mabait ang p-in-atay.
     kind     SM Ci-PV.FN-kill
     'The one who was killed was kind.'
  c. Pulubi ang p-in-atay
     beggar SM Ci-PV.FN-kill
     'The one who was killed was a beggar.'

It is to be noted that in the examples in (3) below, *ang* can occur before not only content words but also function words.

(3) a. Si Lita ang nasa bahay.
     PN Lita SM inside house
     'It is Lita who is at home.'
  b. Ang libro ang sa kaniya.
     DET book SM to him/her
     'It is the book that belongs to him/her.'

Himmelmann (2005: 361) describes the categories of content words along the same lines as Gil (1993). Illustrating the following example (Himmelmann 2005: 361).

(4) at   ang  pare   at   siya  ay   nag-hintay   **ng   sa-sabi-hin  ng**
 and  SM   priest  and  s/he  TM   AV.FN-wait  ng-P  NB-say-PV  ng-A
 sundalo.
 soldier
 'And the priest and he waited for **what the soldier would say**.'

Himmelman (2005: 361) states that: "voice-marked words, which generally have a verb-like meaning, are not restricted to the predicate function. They may occur in other syntactic functions as well. In the following example [i.e. (4)], the undergoer voice form *sasabihin* 'will be said' functions as the patient argument of the actor voice predicate *naghintay* 'waited for'."

Note, however, that example (4) does not indicate that the form *sasabihin* has a noun-like function. It must be kept in mind that the patient argument nature of the form *sasabihin* comes from the nominalization function of the case marker *ng-P*.

To sum up, it is not the case that Tagalog treats nouns, verbs and adjectives alike. The fact that any word can seemingly appear before and after the particle *ang* comes from the function accompanied by the particle *ang*, along with *ng-A*, *ng-P* and *sa*, all of which can nominalize predicates.

The same applies to the function of *si* in Pancor Ngeno-Ngené Sasak (Indonesian) and *'i'* in Mayrinax Atayal (Taiwan) (Shibatani 2009: 170). Note also that the nominalization function can be observed in the case markers *ga* and *wo* of Classical Japanese, as seen in the following example, taken from Ishigaki (1955).

(5) Tomo   no    enpoo  yori   kitaru  **wo** ...           (Ishigaki 1955: 24)
 friend  GEN  far    from   came   ACC
 'my friend who had come from far away' or 'that my friend had come from far away.'

# Chapter 7

# Categorization of words in Tagalog

## 7.1. How can root words in Tagalog be categorized?

In the preceding chapter, we argued that Tagalog makes a clear distinction between nouns and verbs. But this is not always the case, since their categories sometimes can be made clear in sentences that surface, with the exception of originally noun-like words. This raises the question of word classes in Tagalog. An attempt will be made in this chapter to answer this question in some detail. As is well known, morphemes can be divided into two types: free and bound (Bloomfield 1933). Affixes are examples of bound morphemes, for they cannot occur independently. Free morphemes include nouns, verbs, adjectives, etc. Note, however, that in Tagalog, verbs and adjectives are often produced by the addition of affixes. The forms that cannot occur alone but are used together with affixes are termed **root words**, abbreviated as **RWs**. They are abstract words that are realized as concrete words in actual sentences. To put it another way, it is difficult to categorize root words as nouns, verbs and adjectives, in advance. This is because the categories of root words are made clear only when affixes are attached to them: e.g. *ma-RW* → Adjective or Verbs, *mag-RW* → Verb. In the following section, we shall discuss the categorization of words in relation to *root word* and *affix*.

## 7.2. Root words and affixes

Illustrating the RWs *upó* 'to sit' and *kíta* 'to see', we will explore how they are realized as verbs, nouns, etc. For the sake of simplicity, I glossed them as 'to sit' and 'to see', respectively. From the root words *upó* and *kíta*, the following forms are derived (see English 1986).

(1) a. upó': *upó'*, *pag'upó'*, *úpúan* 'sitting', *iupó'* 'to cause to sit, to seat', *makaupó'* 'to be able to sit up', *maupó'* 'to be seated, to seat (oneself)', *pag'upó'* 'act of sitting down', *palaupó'* 'sedentary', *paupuín* 'to get someone a seat', *umupó'* 'to sit down', *úpúan* 'seat'
   b. kíta: *kíta* 'visible', *ipakíta* 'to show', *makákíta* 'to be able to see', *mákiníkíta* 'to foresee', *mákita* 'to be seen, to see', *magkíta* 'to see someone', *magpakíta* 'to show', […], *pakíta* 'demonstration', […], *pagkákíta* 'observation', *pagkikíta* 'act of seeing someone', *pagpapakíta* 'demonstration, (apparition)'

It seems unlikely that *upó'* and *kíta* appear independently (but cf. (5) and (7a) below). (1a) and (1b) show that they are used together with the affixes.

We shall now turn to *gandá* and *lápit*. These are also taken from English (1986).

(2) a. gandá: *gandá* 'beauty', *gandahán* 'to make something beautiful', *gumandá* 'to become beautiful', *magandá* 'beautiful', *kagandáhan* 'beauty'
   b. lápit: *lápit*, *kalapítan* 'nearness', *ilápit* 'to put something near something or someone', *lapítan*, *lumápit* 'to approach', […], *malápit* 'near'

It is clear that the adjectives *magandá* and *malápit* are derived from the RWs *gandá* and *lápit*, respectively. By infixing *-um-* into the RWs, the verbs *gumandá* and *lumápit* are formed, meaning 'to become beautiful' and 'to approach', respectively.

Next, observe the root words *trabáho* and *pangálan*, which are often considered as nouns (see English 1986).

(3) a. trabáho: *trabáho* 'work', [...], *magtrabáho* 'to work', *matrabáho* 'to be able to do', [...], *pagtrabahúhin* 'to give someone work to do', *papagtrabahúhin* 'to force to work'
   b. pangálan: *pangálan* 'name', *kapangálan* 'namesake', *mángalánan* 'to be given a certain name', *pangalánan* 'to give someone a certain name'

It is important to note that the root words *trabaho* and *pangalan* are independent and are classified as nouns. Other related words in (3a) and (3b) are formed by affixing them.

Examples (1)–(3) indicate that actual words are produced when affixes are attached to root words, whereby certain parts of speech and meanings surface. Ø is also included as an affix, since Tagalog has such adjectives as *gutóm* 'hungry' and *pagód* 'tired', which are related to *gútom* 'hunger' and *págod* 'tiredness', respectively.

## 7.3. The Independence hierarchy

Observe the examples in (4)–(5) below, which show that root words differ in independence.

(4) a. Ang mga sílya at  bankó' ay  mga úpúan.    (English 1986: 1544)
     SM  PL  chair and bench TM PL   thing.to sit on
     'Chairs and benches are seats.'

b. Na-upó' (or Um-upó')  siyá          sa  pinaka-magingháwa-ng  sílya.
                                                                    (English 1986: 1544)
   AV.FN-sit               3SG.NOM  in  most-comfortable-LK  chair
   'He seated himself on the most comfortable chair.'

(5) Ang  tabí-ng-dágat  ay    kíta       lámang  nang    bahagyá'  dáhil    sa  úlap.
    SM   side-LK-sea    TM   visible    only    ADVL    slight    because of fog
    'The shore was barely visible through the fog.'        (English 1986: 338)

It will be clear from the discussion so far that the RWs *upó* and *kíta* cannot be used independently (except in (5) and (7a)), while *pangálan* 'name' and *trabáho* 'work, job' can often be used as nouns without nominal affixes. Thus, it can be assumed that there is a gradation among root words as to the extent to which they are independent. We call this gradation the independence hierarchy.

Table 7–1: Independence hierarchy

| more |   |   |   |   |   | less |
|---|---|---|---|---|---|---|
| noun-like |   |   |   |   |   | verb-like |
| *pangálan* | *trabáho* | [...] | *lápit* | [...] | *kíta* | *upó'* |
| 'name' | 'job' |   | 'nearness' |   | 'visible' | 'sit' |

The examples in (6) below show the meanings and actual usages of the words listed in Table 7–1.

(6) a. Anó-ng    pangálan  mo?
       what-LK   name      2SG.GEN
       'What is your name?'
    b. Anó-ng    trabáho  mo?
       what-LK   work     2SG.GEN

'What is your job?'
b'. Nag-trabáho siyá        nang     lábis        kayá' siyá
　　AV.FN-work 3SG.NOM ADVL excessive so   3SG.NOM
　　na-págod.                                    (English 1986: 1452)
　　AV.FN-tired
　　'S/he overworked and so s/he became tired.'
c. Ma-lápit    sa Maynílà' ang  Quezon City.
　　ADJ-near to Manila   SM Quezon City
　　'Quezon City is near Manila.'
d. Na-kíta       ko         siyá         kahápon.
　　PV.FN-see 1SG.ng-A 3SG.NOM yesterday
　　'I saw him/her yesterday.'
e. Um-upó'     kayó.
　　AV.IMP-sit 2PL.NOM
　　'Please sit down.'

The following examples justify that the independent hierarchy obtains.

(7) a. Upó' ka.
　　　sit   2SG.NOM
　　　'Please sit down.'
　　　(This example is informal, often used to direct children to sit.)
　　b. Um-upó'   akó         sa isá-ng     sílya.      (English 1986: 1544)
　　　AV.FN-sit 1SG.NOM on one-LK  chair
　　　'I sat on a chair.'

(8) a. *Trabáho ka.
　　　 job       2SG.NOM
　　　 'Please work.'

b. Mag-trabáho    ka          nang    masípag.
   AV.IMP-work   2SG.NOM   ADVL   diligent
   'Please work hard.'

It is important to note that examples (7) and (8) show that root words with noun-like properties can not be used as verbs without verbal affixes. To conclude, the independence hierarchy suggests that *upó* is more verb-like, whereas *trabáho* is more noun-like.

# Chapter 8

# Linker

## 8.1. Introduction

The linker -*ng*/*na* is used to connect a modifier and a modifiee. (Their order is not relevant here.) The combinations in which the linker are needed are Adjective + Noun, Head Noun + Relative Clause (RC), etc., where the function of the linker is equivalent to the symbol +. That is to say, the linker is used to extend NPs. It can also be used to connect Adjective$_i$ + Adjective$_i$ to emphasize the meaning of the adjective and to form a compound noun of the type Noun + Noun. Furthermore, the linker plays other roles than those mentioned above. In Section 8.2, we will describe how the linker works in the combinations A + N, N + N and A$_i$ + A$_i$. The combination of Head Noun + RC and other related combinations will be dealt with in the next chapter.

## 8.2. Uses of the linker

### 8.2.1. Adjective + Noun or Noun + Adjective

The linker between an adjective and a noun is used to enlarge NPs. Examples of this type are illustrated in (1) through (4) below. I use the hyphen to separate the linker -*ng* pronounced [ŋ] from the preceding word, although it is not used orthographically. When it cannot be separated, I gloss the linker as the sequence .LK, as in *hanging* (wind.LK < hangin-ng). (Number is not relevant to nouns. Nouns can represent both SG and PL without the particle *mga* pronounced [maŋá] that explicitly indicates plurality.)

( 1 ) a. magandá-ng  bulaklák
      beautiful-LK  flower
      'beautiful flower'
   b. bulaklák  na  magandá
      flower  LK  beautiful
      'beautiful flower'

( 2 ) a. mabaít  na  gúro'/títser
      kind  LK  teacher
      'kind teacher'
   b. gúro-ng  mabaít
      teacher-LK  kind
      'kind teacher'

( 3 ) a. malakás  na  hángin                 (BT: 24) (NB: -ng- [ŋ])
      strong  LK  wind
      'strong wind'
   b. hánging  malakás                     (NB: -ng(-) [ŋ])
      wind.LK  strong
      'strong wind'

( 4 ) a. malusóg  na  báta'
      healthy  LK  child

'healthy child'
b. báta-ng    malusóg
   child-LK   healthy
   'healthy child'

As is clear from the examples above, the order of adjective and noun is not relevant. Note that the linker has two allomorphs, i.e. -*ng*/*na*. *Na* appears after words ending in consonants other than the glottal stop /ʔ/, whereas -*ng* appears after words ending in vowels and the glottal stop. When words end in the glottal stop, the glottal stop drops and the allomorph -*ng* is added to the preceding word, as indicated by *gúro-ng* and *báta-ng* in (2b) and (4b), respectively. As seen in (3b), when words end in the dental nasal /n/, this /n/ is replaced by the velar nasal allomorph -*ng*, which is orthographically represented by adding *g* to the preceding *n*.

Note, however, that in some cases, the order of adjective and noun is fixed, as seen below.

(5) a. magandá-ng    umága
       beautiful-LK   morning
       'Good morning.'
    b.*umága-ng      magandá
       morning-LK    beautiful

In the combination of an adjective and a noun, the adjective tends to precede the noun.

### 8.2.2.   Noun + Noun

The linker can be used to form compound nouns of the type N + N. This too is a strategy for the expansion of NPs. We shall now illustrate this type of compound noun with examples.

(6) tabí-ng   dágat
    side-LK   sea
    'beach'

(7) dayúhang          estudyánte
    foreign(er).LK    student
    'foreign student'
    (NB: *Dayuhan* has functions as both a noun 'foreigner' and an adjective 'foreign'.)

(8) báta-ng    babáe
    child-LK   female
    'girl'

### 8.2.3. Adjective$_i$ + Adjective$_i$

As mentioned in Section 8.1, the linker can be used between Adjective$_i$ and Adjective$_j$. The subscript $_{(i)}$ means that the two adjectives are identical. This use of the linker contributes to semantic emphasis on the adjective involved, as seen below.

(9) a. magandá-ng    magandá
       beautiful-LK  beautiful
       'very beautiful'
    b. táma-ng   táma'
       right-LK  right
       'absolutely correct'
    c. masípag  na   masípag
       diligent LK   diligent

'very diligent'

## 8.3. Complementizer: that in English

The linker also serves as a complementizer like English *that*. See examples (10)–(13), which show that Tagalog can do without an empty subject like *it* in English.

(10) Ngayón, tiyák *na* táyo ay ma-gu-gútom.
now certain that 1PL.INCL.NOM TM AV-NB-hungry
'Now, it is certain that we will get hungry.' 'Certainly, we will get hungry.'
(Si Jack at ang puno' ng bitsuwelas: 10)

(11) Na-ísip ni Jack *na* maínam magka-roón ng
PV.FN-think PN.SG.ng-A Jack LK nice AV.NT-get ng-P
enkantádo-ng bitsuwélas.
enchanted-LK bean
'Jack thought that it was nice to get enchanted beans.'
(Si Jack at ang puno' ng bitsuwelas: 8)

(12) S-in-ábi rin ng enkantáda-*ng* siyá ang
Ci-PV.FN-say also ng-A enchanted.woman-LK 3SG.NOM SM
nag-palít ng bitsuwélas sa báka ng mag-iná.
AV.FN-change ng-P bean into cow GEN mother-and-daughter
'The enchanted woman also said that it was she who exchanged enchanted
beans for the cows.' (Si Jack at ang puno' ng bitsuwelas: 50)

(13) Nag-yáya' ang amá-ng óso *na* silá ay
AV.FN-induce SM father-LK bear LK 3PL.NOM TM

um-uwí'.
AV.NT-go.home
'The father bear said, "Let's go home".'

(Si Goldilocks at ang tatlong oso: 42)

Note that examples (10)–(13) have embedded clauses. It is useful to depict the sentence structures in order to have a full understanding of these sentences.

## 8.4. Other uses of the linker

### 8.4.1. Demonstrative pronoun + noun

(14) a. ang    buhók   *na*    itó
      DET   hair    LK   this
      'this (person's) hair'

    b. itó-*ng*    buhók   (*na* itó)
      this-LK   hair     (LK this)
      'this (person's) hair'

Examples (14a) and (14b) show that the linker is used to connect a demonstrative pronoun and a noun. Interestingly enough, a noun can be sandwiched between the two demonstratives, as in (14b).

### 8.4.2. Sentential adverbs/adjectives

The linker serves to integrate an adverb into a clause. For the use of adverbs, see Chapter 24.

(15) Masípag     siyá-*ng*        nag-áral     kahápon.
     industrious   3SG.NOM-LK   AV.FN-study   yesterday
     'S/he studied very hard yesterday.'

### 8.4.3. Auxiliary-like verbs + sentence
In example (16), *gusto* is temporarily treated as Auxiliary.

(16) Gustó ko-*ng* k-um-áin ng mga papáya.
 like 1SG.ng-A-LK Ci-AV.NT-eat ng-P PL papaya
 'I want to eat papayas.'

### 8.4.4. The linker *na* to make word boundaries clear
(17) a. Gustó ni John na mag-áral ng Tagálog.
 like PN.SG.ng-A John LK AV.NT-study ng-P Tagalog
 'John wants to study Tagalog.'
 b. Gustó ni Johng mag-áral ng Tagálog.
 like PN.SG.ng-A John.LK AV.NT-study ng-P Tagalog
 'John wants to study Tagalog.'

See example (17a), which is more commonly used than (17b). This is because the former makes it clear who wants to study; it is not Joh, but John.

## 8.5. Uses of the linker: summary
Further examples are given below, which serve to gain a better understanding of the functions of the linker. Consider which function each example has.

(18) a. B-um-a-bása akó ng libró-ng s-in-úlat
 C$_i$-AV-UF-read 1SG.NOM ng-P book-LK Ci-PV.FN-write
 ni Rizál.
 PN.SG.ng-A Rizal
 'I am reading a book which Rizal wrote.'

b. Na-kíta ko ang estudyánte-ng mulá' sa Hapón.
   PV.FN-see 1SG.ng-A SM student-LK from Japan
   'I saw the student who was from Japan.'

(19) a. Magandá ang bulaklák na itó.
       beautiful SM flower LK this
       'This flower is beautiful.'

   b. Magandá itó-ng bulaklák (na itó).
      beautiful this-LK flower (LK this)
      'This flower is beautiful.'

(20) a. H-in-a-hánap mo ba si Óscar na anák
       Ci-PV-UF-look.for 2SG.ng-A Q SM Oscar LK child
       ni Mang Serafin?                          (MT: 167)
       PN.SG.GEN Serafin
       'Are you looking for Oscar, the son of Serafin?'

   b. Dal-hín mo ang mga gúlay      (*dalhin* < *dala-hin*)
      bring-IMP.PV 2SG.ng-A SM PL vegetable
      kay Miss Réyes na títser ni Renáto.
                                                 (MT: 167)
      PN.SG.DAT Miss Reyes LK teacher PN.SG.GEN Renato
      'Please bring the vegetables to Ms Reyes, who is Renato's teacher.'

(21) a. Mínsan isá-ng panahón, may isá-ng bálo na í-isá ang anák.
       once one-LK time exist one-LK widow LK only-one SM child
       'Once upon a time, there lived a widow who had only one child.'
                            (Si Jack at ang puno' ng bitsuwelas: 4)

   b. I-pa-palít ko sa iyó-ng báka ang mga
      PV-NB-change 1SG.ng-A into 2SG-LK cow SM PL

| | | | | | | |
|---|---|---|---|---|---|---|
| mahiwága-ng | bitsuwélas | na | ibá-ibá | ang | kúlay. | |
| enchanted-LK | bean | LK | various | SM | color | |

'I will exchange the enchanted beans that have various colors for your cow.' (Si Jack at ang puno' ng bitsuwelas: 8)

## Chapter 9

## Relative clause constructions

## 9.1. Introduction

This chapter deals with the sequence of head (H) + relative clause (RC), which is termed the relative clause construction (RCC). As the symbol + indicates, the linker serves to relate the head and the relative clause.

## 9.2. Structure of relative clause constructions

Relative clause constructions (i.e. H + RC or RC + H) consist of a modified noun (i.e. Head) and a modifier (i.e. RC). It is clear that the combination of a relative clause with a head noun is parallel to the combination of an adjective with a noun, because a relative clause corresponds to a modifier and a head to a modified noun. The resulting construction as a whole is termed a relative clause construction (RCC), where **relative** means that the head and the RC can be related to each other. The (b) structures below are examples of RCCs.

( 1 ) a. B-um-ilí       ng    mga manggá ang laláki.
       Ci-AV.FN-buy ng-P  PL    mango   SM  man

'The man bought mangoes.'
b. ang    laláki-ng b-um-ilí         ng    mga manggá
   DET   man-LK   Ci-AV.FN-buy   ng-P  PL   mango
   'the man who bought mangoes'

(2) a. B-um-ása         ng    libró ang estudyánte.
       Ci-AV.FN-read  ng-P  book  SM  student
       'The student read a book.'
    b. ang    estudyánte-ng b-um-ása         ng    libró
       DET   student-LK    Ci-AV.FN-read  ng-P  book
       'the student who read a book'

(3) a. B-in-ása         ng    estudyánte ang libró.
       Ci-PV.FN-read  ng-A  student    SM  book
       'The student read the book.'
    b. ang    libró-ng b-in-ása         ng    estudyánte
       DET   book-LK  Ci-PV.FN-read  ng-A  student
       'the book that the student read'

(4) a. B-in-il-hán         ni          Pédro ng    tinápay ang tindáhan.
       Ci-FN-buy-LV   PN.SG.ng-A  Pedro ng-P  bread   SM  store
       'Pedro bought some bread at the store.'
    b. ang    tindáhang b-in-il-hán         ni          Pédro ng    tinápay
       DET   store.LK   Ci-FN-buy-LV   PN.SG.ng-A  Pedro ng-P  bread
       'the store at which Pedro bought some bread'   (*binilhan* < *b-in-ili-han*)

Note that the particle *ng* is, in some cases, glossed as ng-P, while in other cases it is glossed as ng-A. This has been discussed in Chapter 1, where I have proposed that Tagalog has two types of *ng* because they differ in function. In fact, *ng-P* can be treated as the accusative case marker and *ng-A* as the genitive case marker in terms of the accusative analysis, although linguists tend to treat them alike as the genitive or ergative case marker, or simply as *ng*-forms. Note, in passing, that in (4) above, the voice-related suffix *-han* agrees with the nominal suffix *tindahan* 'store', which implies that *-(h)an* originally denoted the place where actions related to RWs take place. *Tinda* 'goods for sale' is a borrowing from Spanish *tienda* (English 1986: 1421).

## 9.3. Subject-sensitive relative clause formation

Now observe examples (5)–(6).

(5) a. B-um-ilí          ng    mga manggá ang laláki. (= (1a))
       Ci-AV.FN-buy  ng-P  PL   mango   SM  man
       'The man bought mangoes.'
    b. ang   laláki-ng [b-um-ilí        ng    mga manggá]
       DET  man-LK  Ci-AV.FN-buy ng-P  PL   mango
       'the man who bought some mangoes'
    c.*ang  mga manggá-ng [b-um-ilí         ang laláki]
       DET  PL  mango-LK  Ci-AV.FN-buy  SM  man
       Intended: 'the mangoes that the man bought'

(6) a. B-in-ása          ng    estudyánte ang libró. (= (3a))
       Ci-PV.FN-read  ng-A  student      SM  book
       'The student read the book.'
    b. ang   libró-ng [b-in-ása         ng    estudyánte]
       DET  book-LK Ci-PV.FN-read ng-A  student
       'the book that the student bought'

    c.*ang   libró-ng  [b-um-ása     *ang* estudyánte]
       DET  book-LK  Ci-AV.FN-read  SM  student
       Intended: 'the book that the student read'

Note that (5c) and (6c) are ungrammatical, despite the fact that the English equivalents are grammatical. Now compare the grammatical RCCs and the ungrammatical RCCs to see what is crucial for the grammaticality of RCCs. It is interesting to note that the ungrammatical RCs involve *ang NP* (cf. (5c) and (6c)), while the grammatical ones do not (cf. (5b) and (6b)). Thus, we reach the conclusion that RCs are not permitted to include *ang NP* (i.e. subject NP). We will call this constraint the **subject constraint**, because it reflects the strategy that NPs relativized on must be subject NPs or *ang*-phrases. Incidentally, the subject constraint is a typological characteristic of Western Austronesian languages (cf. Keenan and Comrie 1977).

It seems likely that Tagalog does not have a full range of expressive power, because it relativizes on subject NPs only. Recall, however, that the voice variation system enables core and peripheral arguments to be promoted as subjects.

## 9.4. Order of relative clause and head

As mentioned in the preceding chapter, the order of modifier and modifiee is not relevant. That is, Modifier + Modifiee and Modifiee + Modifier are both allowable. This also applies to RCC formation. That is, both the H + RC order and the RC + H order are theoretically permissible. The following are examples of both orders of RCCs.

( 7 ) a. babáe-ng   [nag-ba-bása  ng    dyáryo]        (Comrie 1981: 141)
      woman-LK  AV-UF-read  ng-P  newspaper
      'a woman who is reading a newspaper'

b. [nag-ba-bása ng dyáryo]-ng babáe  (Comrie 1981: 141)
   AV-UF-read ng-P newspaper-LK woman
   'a woman who is reading a newspaper'

(8) a. ang libró-ng [nása mésa]
    DET book-LK on table
    'the book that is on the table'
  b. ang [nása mésa]-ng libró
    DET on table-LK book
    'the book that is on the table'

(9) a. Naka-ka-kíta kamí ng babáe-ng [s-um-a-sayáw].
    AV-UF-see 1PL.EXCL.NOM ng-P woman-LK $C_i$-AV-UF-dance
    'We see a girl who is dancing.'
  b. Naka-ka-kíta kamí ng [s-um-a-sayáw] na babáe.
    AV-UF-see 1PL.EXCL.NOM ng-P $C_i$-AV-UF-dance LK woman
    'We see a dancing girl.'

Theoretically, it seems possible that either order occurs indiscriminately. However, this is not always the case. The H + RC order may be preferable, partly because the order is more readily perceptible when the RC is longer. Comparing (7b) with (9b) above, native speakers of Tagalog suggest that (7b) exemplified by Comrie (1981: 141) is not acceptable, while (9b) is acceptable. This is because in (9b) the RC is short, just the verb form [*sumásayáw*]. Thus, it turns out that the order of H and RC has to do with perceptibility. In VO languages, the H + RC order is generally preferred cross-linguistically.

## 9.5. Special types of relative clause construction

In this chapter, we have dealt with relative clause constructions where the linker necessarily appears. The function of the linker dealt with in the preceding chapter, along with the function of RCC formation, is regarded as the **connective** function, because it serves to connect two forms. In what follows, we shall illustrate other functions than those dealt with so far.

### 9.5.1. Possessive relativization

It is to be noted that even the possessor can be relativized on, as seen in (10) and (11) below.

(10) Mínsan isá-ng panahón, may tatló-ng laláki-ng kambíng
 once one-LK time exist three-LK male-LK goat
 na [ang pangálan ay Grap].
 LK SM name TM Grap
 'Once upon a time, there lived three he-goats *whose* names were Grap.'
 (Ang Tatlong Grap na Lalaking Kambing: 4)

(11) Na-ga-gálit ang áking iná sa mga báta-*ng*
 AV-UF-angry SM 1SG.GEN.LK mother with PL child-LK
 [matigás ang úlo].
 hard SM head
 'My mother is angry with (her) hard-headed children.' (BT: 55)

Note that in (10) and (11) above, an *ang*-marked NP does appear in the embedded relative clauses. This implies that a strategy different from what has been mentioned thus far works in possessor relativization.

## 9.5.2. Apposition

Examples (12)–(15) below show that RCCs in Tagalog have the structure $H_i$ + $RC_j$, in which $RC_j$ is appositive to the preceding $H_i$. By appositive it is meant that $RC_j$ represents the content of $H_i$. The symbol + in the structure $H_i$ + $RC_j$ symbolizes the linker. Note that this structure is similar to the *the fact that S* construction in English.

(12) S-um-ang'áyon si John sa proposisyon [*na* mag-pa-dalá
    Ci-AV.FN-agree SM John with proposition LK AV.NT-CAUS-bring
    ng delegation sa Malakaniyáng]. (MT: 167)
    ng-P delegation to Malakaniyang Palace
    'John agreed with the proposition that they send a delegation to Malakaniang.'

(13) Si Nánay ay um-a-áyon sa áking náis
    SM mother TM AV-UF-sympathise with 1SG.GEN.LK wish
    [*na* magíng doktór]. (English 1986: 93)
    LK NT.become doctor
    'Mother sympathizes with my wish to become a doctor.'

(14) Ang balíta' [*na* u-uwí' si Dexter sa summer] ang
    DET news LK AV.NB-come.home SM Dexter in summer SM
    nag-pa-sayá sa Tátay. (MT: 168)
    AV.FN-CAUS-happy DAT father
    'What made his (Dexter's) father happy is the news that Dexter will return home this summer.'

### 9.5.3. Relative adverbs

The linker is also used to form the relative adverb construction, when the head is the form that represents the place, time and manner related to the action or event. See (15) below, where the clause headed by the *ang N* form modifies the head noun *panahón* 'time'. This type of construction is structurally parallel to the appositive construction. Overall, RCCs consist of H + RC, whereby the H form plays a crucial role in determining whether the RCC at issue functions as an appositive RC or a relative adverb construction. These distinctions cannot be made formally in Tagalog, because *ang-NP* is allowable in both appositive RCs and relative adverbs.

(15) At    d-um-atíng           ang  panahón  na  ang  réyna  ay
     and   Ci-AV.FN-arrive  SM   time       LK   SM   queen  TM
     nagka-anák              ng    isá-ng    sanggól  na  babáe.
     AV.FN.have-child    ng-P  one-LK   baby        LK  girl
     'And then, the time came when the queen gave birth to a girl baby.'
     (Si Snow White at ang pitong duwende: 4)

### 9.5.4. Head internal relative clause constructions

As mentioned before, Tagalog RCCs have two orders: Head + RC and RC + Head. Interestingly, the RC + Head order produces a head-internal RCC, as shown in (16b).

(16) a. Itó   ang  sílya-ng   [s-in-íra'                ng     laláki].
        this  SM   chair-LK  Ci-PV.FN-destroy  ng-A  man
        'This is the chair that the man destroyed.'
     b. Itó   ang  [s-in-íra-*ng*                [*sílya*]  ng     laláki].
        this  SM   Ci-PV.FN-destroy-LK   chair     ng-A  man
        'This is the chair that the man destroyed.'

# Part II

Verbs and Morphology

# Chapter 10

# Agent voice 1: *-um-* verbs

## 10.1.   What is the agent voice?

The term agent voice (AV) means that an agent NP plays the subject role in a simple sentence. Agent-voiced sentences can be identified by the verb forms marked with *-um-* and *mag-*. An experiencer NP can also be treated as an agent NP, in view of its marking on verbs. This chapter deals with agent-voiced (AV) sentences whose verb stems are marked by *-um-* (called **-um- verbs**, hereafter). Another type of agent-voiced sentences will be dealt with in the next chapter.

The following are sentences whose verb stems are marked by *-um-*.

( 1 ) a. P-um-untá    siyá        sa Mayníla' kahápon.
     Ci-AV.FN-go 3SG.NOM  to Manila   yesterday
     'S/he went to Manila yesterday.'

  b. K-um-áin      akó         ng    balót kagabí.
     Ci-AV.FN-eat 1SG.NOM  ng-P  balot last.night
     'I ate a balot last night.'

  c. Um-i-inóm    ng    saríwa-ng gátas ang mga báta' áraw-áraw.
     AV-UF-drink ng-P  fresh-LK  milk  SM  PL  child everyday

'The children drink fresh milk everyday.'

Note that these examples have agent subjects (i.e. *siya*, *ako* and *ang mga bata*, respectively) and their subject status can be identified by the verbal affix (-)*um*-.

## 10.2. Conjugation pattern of -um- verbs

This section shows the conjugation pattern of *-um-* verbs, along with the position of stress. As mentioned in Chapter 7, it is difficult to predetermine the categories of RWs in advance. This is because categories of RWs become clear only when they are actually used together with affixes: *ma*-RW → Adjective, *mag*-RW → Verb, etc. See Table 10–1 below, which makes it clear that which RW takes -um- is predetermined. Note that in the conjugation of *-um-* verbs, regularities can be found in morphology and accentuation.

Table 10–1: Conjugation pattern of -um- verbs

| Root Word | puntá 'to go' | káin 'to eat' | inóm 'to drink' | Gloss |
|---|---|---|---|---|
| Neutral | p-um-untá | k-um-áin | um-inóm | (Ci)-AV.NT-RW |
| Imperative | p-um-untá | k-um-áin | um-inóm | (Ci-)AV.IMP-RW |
| Perfective | p-um-untá | k-um-áin | um-inóm | (Ci-)AV.FN-RW |
| Imperfective | p-um-ú-puntá | k-um-a-káin | um-í-inóm | (Ci-)AV-UF-RW |
| Inceptive | pú-puntá | ka-káin | í-inóm | (Ci)AV.NB-RW |

Let us first discuss the morphological regularities. Accentuation of *-um-* verbs will be discussed in Section 10.5.

As is clear from Table 10–1, the conjugation of *-um-* verbs is rule-governed. The neutral, imperative and perfective forms are identical. (The neutral form functionally corresponds to the infinitive in English.) They are formed by putting *-um-* before the first vowel of RWs (Ramos and Cena 1990: 48). The inceptive form is produced by reduplicating the first (C)V of RWs. The imperfective forms are produced by putting -*um*- before the first vowel of the inceptive forms.

It is worth mentioning here that Tagalog uses the imperfective form when English uses the past progressive form, as seen in (2). This comes from the fact that the verbal conjugation in Tagalog is patterned according to the aspectual system.

( 2 ) Nag-lu-lúto' ng pagkáin ang nánay noóng d-um-atíng
AV-**UF**-cook ng-P food SM mother when.LK C$_i$-AV.FN-arrive
akó.
1SG.NOM
'Mother was cooking some food when I arrived.'
(Schachter and Otanes 1972: 67)

Note that the imperfective form represents both an action in progress and a habitual action. See the examples in (3a) and (3b) below, where the former is progressive and the latter is habitual.

( 3 ) a. S-um-u-súlat akó ng líham ngayón.
C$_i$-AV-**UF**-write 1SG.NOM ng-P letter now
'I am writing a letter **now**.'
b. S-um-u-súlat akó ng líham sa áking nánay
C$_i$-AV-**UF**-write 1SG.NOM ng-P letter to 1SG.GEN.LK mother
tuwí-ng Línggo.
every-LK Sunday
'I write a letter to my mother **every Sunday**.'

When we need to express the action in progress, the following expressions can be used (p.c. Ms furuya). Compare (4a-b) with (5).

(4) a. **Pa**-puntá (na) ako sa eskuwelahán.
    AV-go (now) 1SG.NOM to school
    'I am now going to school.'
  b. **Pa**-datíng silá sa ákin.
    AV-arrive 3PL.NOM to school
    'They are approaching me.'

(5) P-um-u-puntá akó sa eskuwelahán áraw-áraw.
    Ci-AV-UF-go 1SG.NOM to school every day
    'I go to school every day.'

It is not the case that every -*um*- verb makes this distinction. It is lexically determined (p.c. Manueli, Feb. 28, 2005), where it is assumed that the prefix **pa**- accompanies verbs of motion.

(6) a. K-um-a-káin akó ng tanghalían.
    Ci-AF-UF-eat 1SG.NOM ng-P lunch
    'I am now eating lunch.'
  b.*Pa-káin akó ng tanghalían.
    AV-eat 1SG.NOM ng-P lunch
    Intended: 'I am now eating lunch.'

## 10.3. Description of aspectual features

The aspects of verbs in Tagalog can be described in terms of its features [±Begun] and [±Finished], as shown in Table 10–2.

Let us now turn our attention to reduplication. It seems that reduplication (RED) in Tagalog may be correlated with the feature [–finished]. In fact, reduplication is found in the imperfective and inceptive forms. (7) shows how the

Table 10–2: Feature description of aspects

| Aspects | ±Begun | ±Finished | RED |
|---|---|---|---|
| Neutral | – | – | – |
| Imperative | – | – | – |
| Perfective | + | + | – |
| Imperfective | + | – | + |
| Inceptive | – | – | + |

perfective, imperfective and inceptive forms can be analyzed.

( 7 ) a. Perfective: +Begun [BG], +Finished [**FN**]   (FN: finished)
    b. Imperfective: +Begun [BG], –Finished [**UF**]   (UF: unfinished)
    c. Inceptive: –Begun [**NB**], (–Finished [UF])   (NB: not-begun)

Thus, it is convenient to gloss the perfect, imperfective and inceptive forms as [FN], [UF] and [NB], respectively. See (8a) and (8b) below.

( 8 ) a. P-um-untá         akó         sa eskuwelahán kahápon.
      Ci-AV.**FN**-go  1SG.NOM  to school         yesterday
      'I went to school yesterday.'
    b. P-um-u-puntá akó         sa eskuwelahán áraw-áraw.
      $C_i$-AV-**UF**-go  1SG.NOM  to school         every day
      'I go to school everyday.'
    c. Pu-puntá    akó         sa eskuwelahán búkas.
      AV.**NB**-go 1SG.NOM  to school         tomorrow
      'I will go to school tomorrow.'

Note that reduplication correctly predicts that the action is not finished. The inceptive form indicates that the action has not begun yet.

## 10.4. Uses of neutral forms

The neutral forms are produced by placing *-um-* just before the first vowel of the RWs. See examples (9a) and (9b) below, which show that *l-um-akí* 'to become big' and *l-um-ápit* 'to approach' are derived from *lakí* 'bigness' and *lápit* 'nearness', respectively.

(9) a. *ma-lakí* 'big', *l-um-akí* 'to grow', *l-um-á-lakí* (IMPF), *lá-lakí* (INCP)
   b. *ma-lápit* 'near', *l-um-ápit* 'to approach', *l-um-a-lápit* (IMPF), *la-lápit* (INCP)

We are now in a position to explain how the neutral forms are used. In example (10) below, the neutral form *k-um-áin* 'to eat' is used in an embedded clause headed by the auxiliary-like verb *áyaw* 'to dislike'. This use is similar to the infinitive in English, as the translation equivalent indicates. This form is termed 'neutral' in the sense that it does not represent a specific aspect.

(10) Áyaw    ko-ng         k-um-áin        ng    balót.
     dislike 1SG.ng-A-LK   Ci-AV.NT-eat    ng-P  balot
     'I don't want to eat a balot.'

## 10.5. Accentuation of -um- verbs

In this section, we shall consider the accentuation of *-um-* verbs. Keep in mind that the stress of RWs cannot be predicted. Therefore, the position of stress in RWs must be memorized. Note, however, that the additional stress accompanied by the conjugation of *-um-* verbs can be predicted if we know the position of stress in RWs, as mentioned briefly in Chapter 2 ('Phonology').

The RWs that consist of $S_2S_1$# have two types of accentuation, as shown below.

(11) a. $S_2\acute{S}_1\#$
   b. $\acute{S}_2 S_1\#$
   (#: word boundary, Ś: stressed syllable, S: unstressed syllable)

*Puntá* 'to go' and *inóm* 'to drink' are examples of (11a), and *káin* 'eat' is an example of (11b). *Puntá* and *káin* conjugate as follows:

(12) a. p-um-untá [pu/mun/tá], p-um-ú-puntá [pu/mú/pun/tá], pú-puntá [pú/pun/tá]
   b. k-um-áin [ku/má/'in], k-um-a-káin [ku/ma/ká/'in], ka-káin [ka/ká/'in]
   (The symbol / represents syllable boundary.)

It is clear from (12) that the $S_2\acute{S}_1\#$ type conjugates as $\acute{S}_3 S_2 \acute{S}_1\#$, and the $\acute{S}S\#$ type as $S_3\acute{S}_2 S_1\#$. In dictionaries, the type (12b) is sometimes described as $\acute{S}_3\acute{S}_2 S_1\#$ (e.g. kákáin). Note, however, that **the $\acute{S}_3$ is not so prominent as the $\acute{S}_2$**. Thus, we ignore the $\acute{S}_3$ of the $\acute{S}_2 S_1\#$ type in what follows.

Thus, verbal accentuation of the $S_2\acute{S}_1\#$ type and the $\acute{S}_2 S_1\#$ type can be formulated as follows:

(13) a. $S_2\acute{S}_1\# \rightarrow (\acute{S}_3)S_2\acute{S}_1\#$
   b. $\acute{S}_2 S_1\# \rightarrow$ Vacant

If we take reduplication into account, the following rules alternatively obtain. RED involves an initial (C)V of the RW.

(14) a. $S_2\acute{S}_1\# \rightarrow (\text{RÉD})S_2\acute{S}_1\#$
   b. $\acute{S}_2 S_1\# \rightarrow$ Vacant

# Chapter 11

# Agent voice 2: *mag-* verbs

## 11.1. Agent-voiced: mag- verbs

In the preceding chapter, we mentioned that there are two types of agent voice (AV) and discussed the AV of the *-um-* verb type. In this chapter, we shall deal with another type of AV, which involves the type of sentences whose verb forms are marked by the prefix *mag-* (called ***mag-* verbs**, hereafter). As mentioned in the preceding chapter, sentences with the experiencer subject are also treated as agent-voiced. The following are examples in which the *mag-* verbs are used. Note that their subjects are all agents.

(1) Nag-la-laró' ang mga báta' ngayón.
    AV-UF-play SM PL child now
    'The children are playing now.'

(2) Nag-lúto' ng isdá' ang áking iná.
    AV.FN-cook ng-P fish SM 1SG.GEN.LK mother
    'My mother cooked fish.'

(3) Mag-áral        táyo                ng    Tagálog áraw-áraw.
    AV.IMP-study 1PL.INCL.NOM ng-P Tagalog everyday
    'Let us learn Tagalog everyday.'

Keep in mind that we cannot predict which RWs occur with -*um*- or *mag*-. In other words, whether a particular RW takes -*um*- or *mag*- is lexically determined. Exceptionally, some RWs can take either, some without changing meaning (e.g. *lumákad/maglakád* 'to walk'), others with a change of meaning (e.g. *l-um-abás* 'to go out'/*mag-labás* 'to take out something, to withdraw (money)'). For more information on the use of -*um*- and *mag*-, see Pittman (1996) and Ramos (1974).

## 11.2. Conjugation pattern of mag- verbs

The conjugation and accentuation of *mag*-verbs are shown in Table 11–1. The conjugation pattern of *mag*- is almost the same as that of -*um*- verbs (see (4c) below). The only difference is that -*um*- is an infix and *mag*- a prefix.

Table 11–1: Conjugation and accentuation patterns of *mag*- verbs

| Root Word | laró' 'to play' | salitá' 'to speak' | áral 'to study' | Gloss |
|---|---|---|---|---|
| Neutral | mag-laró' | mag-salitá' | mag-áral | AV.NT-RW |
| Imperative | mag-laró' | mag-salitá' | mag-áral | AV.IMP-RW |
| Perfective | nag-laró' | nag-salitá' | nag-áral | AV.FN-RW |
| Imperfective | nag-lá-laró' | nag-sá-salitá' | nag-a-áral | AV.UF-RW |
| Inceptive | mag-lá-laró' | mag-sá-salitá' | mag-a-áral | AV.NB-RW |

Some notes on the conjugation pattern of *mag*- verbs are in order.

(4) Notes on the conjugation pattern of *mag*- verbs
    a. The perfective forms of *mag*- verbs are produced by changing *mag*-

into <u>n</u>ag-.
b. The imperfective forms are produced by changing <u>m</u>ag- into <u>n</u>ag- and reduplicating the first (C)V of RWs.
c. The perfective form is different from the neutral and imperative forms, in contrast to that of -*um*- verbs.
d. *Nag*- indicates that the action has already begun (i.e. realis), whereas *mag*- indicates that the action has not begun yet (i.e. irrealis).
e. Reduplication shows that the action expressed by an RW is not finished.

Incidentally, the inceptive forms of -*um*- and *mag*- verbs are often used instead of their imperative forms in order to weaken the nuance of coercion.

## 11.3. Accentuation of mag- verbs

As is clear from the examples *maglaró*/*naglálaró* and *mag'áral*/*nag'aáral*, the accentual rules of -*um*- verbs apply to *mag*- verbs without any modification. See the rules in (5) below.

(5) a. $S_2\acute{S}_1\# \rightarrow (\acute{S}_3)S_2\acute{S}_1\#$: mag-laró 'to play', mag-lá-laró
  b. $\acute{S}_2S_1\# \rightarrow$ Vacant: mag-áral 'to study', mag-a-áral

(6) a. $S_3S_2\acute{S}_1\# \rightarrow (\acute{S}_4)S_3S_2\acute{S}_1\#$: mag-salitá 'to speak', mag-sá-salitá
  b. $S_3\acute{S}_2S_1\# \rightarrow (\acute{S}_4)S_3\acute{S}_2S_1\#$: mag-trabáho 'to work', mag-t(r)á-tra-báho

When reduplication is taken into considerarion, the rules in (5) and (6) become simple, as (5) and (6) can be collapsed into (7).

(7) a. $(S_3)S_2\acute{S}_1\# \rightarrow (\text{RÉD})(S_3)S_2\acute{S}_1\#$, where the first (C)V of RWs is involved in RÉD.

b. $S_3\acute{S}_2S_1\# \rightarrow (\text{RÉD})S_3\acute{S}_2S_1\#$, where the first (C)V of RWs is involved in RÉD.
c. $\acute{S}_2S_1\# \rightarrow$ Vacant

(7a) and (7b) correctly predict the accentuation of RWs like *salitá'* 'to speak' and *trabáho* 'to work' respectively, both of which consist of more than two syllables. See (8) below.

( 8 ) a. salitá': mag-salitá' → nag-sá-salitá', mag-sá-salitá'
　　　b. trabáho: mag-trabáho → nag-t(r)á-trabáho, mag-t(r)á-trabáho

Thus, the accentuation patterns of both *-um-* and *mag-* verbs can be described in terms of the rules in (7). These rules can also be applied to *ma*-verbs, which will be discussed in Chapter 16.

# Chapter 12

# Patient voice: -*(h)in*

## 12.1. What is the patient voice?

Sentences whose subject plays a patient role are in the patient voice (PV), when the verb forms are marked by the suffix *-(h)in* or by the infix *-in-* (called *-(h)in* **verbs**, hereafter). As seen in Table 12–1 below, *-(h)in* and *-in-* are in complementary distribution. That is, *-(h)in* is used in Irrealis aspects, otherwise *-in-* is used. It is important to note that when a patient NP is *definite*, a PV sentence automatically surfaces, because AV sentences lack a marker for a definite reference in the accusative case. Thus, in a PV sentence, the patient NP serves as the subject and is preceded by *ang*. There is good reason to make a distinction between **ng-A** and **ng-P,** which mark the non-subject agent NP and the non-subject patient NP, respectively, despite the fact that they are represented by the same form *ng* pronounced [naŋ]. This distinction serves to avoid the controversy over accusative/ergative morphology, as mentioned in Chapter 1. See the following examples, where the sentences in (a) are PV and the sentences in (b) are AV.

( 1 ) a. A-awít-in     ng    mga báta' ang 'Báhay Kúbo'.        (BT: 49)
         NB-sing-PV ng-A PL   child SM Bahay Kubo

'The children will sing the song *Bahay Kubo*.'

b. A-áwit      ang mga báta' ng    awit/kantá.
AV.NB-sing SM PL   child ng-P song
'The children will sing a song.'

(2) a. K-in-áin      ng    mga kápitbáhay ko      ang litsón
Ci-PV.FN-eat ng-A PL   neighbor   1SG.GEN SM roast.pig
sa áming       pistá.
in 1PL.EXCL.LK festival
'My neighbors ate the roast pig in our festival.'

b. K-um-áin     ng      litsón    ang mga kápitbáhay ko      sa
Ci-AV.FN-eat ng-P roast.pig SM PL    neighbor    1SG.GEN in
áming       pistá.
1PL.EXCL.LK festival
'My neighbors ate a roast pig in our festival.'

(3) a. Ni-lu-lúto'    ng     katúlong ang isdá.
PV-UF-cook ng-A helper     SM fish
'The helper is cooking the fish.'

b. Nag-lu-lúto' ng    isdá ang katútong.
AV-UF-cook ng-P fish    SM helper
'The helper is cooking fish.'

(4) a. B-in-ilí       ng      áking          amá    ang aklát na gustó
Ci-PV.FN-buy ng-A 1SG.GEN.LK father SM book LK want
ko-ng       basá-hin.
1SG.ng-A-LK read-NT.PV
'My father bought the book that I wanted to read.'

b. B-um-ilí     ang áking        amá    ng    aklát na gustó
   Ci-AV.FN-buy SM  1SG.GEN.LK  father ng-P  book  LK  want
   ko-ng          basá-hin.
   1SG.ng-A-LK  read-NT.PV
   'My father bought a book that I wanted to read.'

(5) a. Ba-basá-hin   ko        ang aklát na  s-in-úlat
      NB-read-PV    1SG.ng-A  SM  book LK   Ci-PV.FN-write
      ni            Dr. Rizál.
      PN.SG.ng-A   Dr. Rizal
      'I'm going to read the book that Dr. Rizal wrote.'
   b. Ba-basá       akó        ng    aklát na  s-in-úlat
      AV.NB-read   1SG.NOM   ng-p  book  LK   Ci-PV.FN-write
      ni            Dr. Rizál.
      PN.SG.ng-A   Dr. Rizal
      'I'm going to read a book that Dr. Rizal wrote.'

(6) a. Anó  ang g-in-a-gawá'    mo?
      what SM  C$_i$-PV-UF-do  2SG.ng-A
      'What are you doing?'
   b.*Anó  ang g-um-a-gawá'  ka?
      what SM  C$_i$-AV-UF-do  2SG.NOM
      Intended: 'What are you doing?'

Recall that patient NPs marked with *ng-P* in AV sentences are indefinite, whereas those in PV sentences marked with *ang* are definite, as the translation equivalents above indicate. This fact is important in explaining why in discourse, PV sentences appear more frequently than AV ones. Ergative analysts of Tagalog maintain that this is one of the properties in favor of ergative morphology.

## 12.2. Conjugation pattern of -(h)in verbs

Now observe the conjugation pattern of *-(h)in* verbs given in Table 12–1.

Table 12–1: Conjugation pattern of *-(h)in* verbs

| Root Word | inóm 'to drink' | bása 'to read' | lúto' 'to cook' | Gloss |
|---|---|---|---|---|
| Neutral | inum-ín | basá-hin | lutú'-in | RW-NT.PV |
| Imperative | inum-ín | basá-hin | lutú'-in | RW-IMP.PV |
| Perfective | in-inóm | b-in-ása | ni-lúto' | (Ci-)PV.FN-RW |
| Imperfective | in-í-inóm | b-in-a-bása | ni-lu-lúto' | (Ci-)PV-UF-RW |
| Inceptive | í-inum-ín | bá-basá-hin | lú-lutú'-in | NB-RW-PV |

The neutral and imperative forms are produced by suffixing *-(h)in* on RWs, when stress shifts to the subsequent syllable. The perfective forms are produced by putting *-in-* immediately before the first vowel of RWs. The inceptive forms are derived by reduplicating the initial (C)V of the neutral forms. The imperfective forms are made by putting *-in-* before the first vowel of the reduplicated forms: e.g. *bása* > *ba-bása* > *b-in-a-bása*. Alternatively, the perfective and imperfective forms have the zero suffix, when the affix *(-)in-* denotes that the action has begun. It seems that to use Ø complicates the morphological analysis of *-(h)in* verbs. Thus, I avoided to use Ø in describing *-(h)in* verbs.

Note that *lúto'* 'cook' is an exception, as will be explained in (7b) below. Reduplication is found in the imperfective and inceptive forms, indicating that an action denoted by an RW is not finished.

To gain a full understanding of the conjugation pattern of *-(h)in* verbs, the following notes are of use (cf. also Aspillera 1969).

( 7 ) a. When a RW ends in a vowel, *h* is inserted between the RW and the suffix *-in*, as in *basáhin*. In the framework of generative phonology, *básah* is assumed as an underlying representation, with the result that all RWs end in a consonant. We do not adopt this assumption, because it is not plausible that each RW deletes the final *-h* when it does not take the suffix.

b. When a RW begins with *l*, *w* or *y*, *ni-*, instead of *-in-*, is prefixed to form the perfective and imperfective forms; see *lúto'*: *l-in-úto'* → *nilúto'* (metathesis, etc.). (Note that some people use *linúto'*.)

c. /o/ in final syllables of RWs is realized as [u] in non-final syllables when the suffix *-(h)in* is attached, as in *nilúto'* and *lutú'in*.

d. When the suffix *-(h)in* is attached to some RWs, the vowel of the root-final syllable is deleted, e.g. *bilhín* < *bili* + *hín* 'buy'. It is not predictable which RWs are involved in this phenomenon. Therefore, we must memorize which RWs undergo this phonological process. Generative phonology usually processes them by using a minor rule like [+Vowel Deletion].

e. *Sundín* 'follow' and *kúnin* 'get' are irregular forms. *Sundín* is formed by applying the vowel deletion just mentioned to the RW *sunód*. *Kúnin* is derived from *kuhá-hin* to which the vowel deletion and other sporadic phonological changes have been applied.

## 12.3. Accentuation of -(h)in verbs

The accentual pattern of *-(h)in* verbs seems quite different from those of *-um-* and *mag-* verbs (but see (8c) below). This section deals with the accentuation characteristic of *-(h)in* verbs.

(8) a. When *-(h)in* is suffixed to a RW, stress shifts to the subsequent syllable.

b. A RW consisting of two syllables with stress on the ultimate syllable has an additional stress on the reduplicated (C)V of its imperfective and inceptive forms.

c. In the imperfective forms, the rules similar to *-um-/mag-* verbs are applicable; see (10a) and (10b) below.

The above can be summarized as follows:

( 9 ) Neutral, Imperative, Inceptive (Irrealis)
   a. $S_2\acute{S}_1 + (h)in\# \rightarrow (RÉD)S_2S_1 + (h)ín\#$
   b. $\acute{S}_2S_1 + (h)in\# \rightarrow (RÉD)S_2\acute{S}_1 + (h)ín\#$

(10) Perfective, Imperfective (Realis)
   a. $S_2\acute{S}_1\# \rightarrow (RÉD)S_2\acute{S}_1\#$
   b. $\acute{S}_2S_1\# \rightarrow$ Vacant

Note finally that in (9) and (10) above, $S_3$ is ignored for the sake of convenience. Thus, RED is substantially $S_2$.

# Chapter 13

# Directional voice: *-(h)an*

## 13.1. Introduction

Verbs marked with the suffix *-(h)an* have various functions; they are used in sentences whose subjects denote roles such as Locative, Source, Directional, Recipient, Benefactive and Patient. In what follows, we will call these verbs *-(h)an* **verbs** and call sentences of this type Directional voice (DV). Thus, DV is the cover term related to the roles just mentioned, where the term DV is based on morphological marking, rather than semantics. This chapter aims to illustrate the functions of *-(h)an* with examples.

### 13.1.1. Locative

In example (1b) below, the subject indicates the place on which the agent wrote his/her name.

( 1 ) a. S-um-úlat      ang báta' (ng     pangálan niyá)        sa aklát.
                                                                  (BT: 93)
   Ci-AV.FN-write  SM child (ng-P name     3SG.GEN) on book
   'The child wrote (his/her name) on the book.'

b. S-in-ulát-an ng báta' (ng pangálan niyá) ang
   C$_i$-FN-write-DV ng-A child (ng-P name 3SG.GEN) SM
   aklát. (BT: 93)
   book
   'The child wrote (his/her name) on the book.'
   (NB: the NP preceded by *ng-P* becomes definite when followed by a definite modifier like *niyá* 'his/her'.)

Note, however, that Ramos (1974: 127) suggests that when the agent uses something to do an action, the *pag-Vst-an* form is sometimes used, as seen in (2b) below.

( 2 ) a. S-in-ulátan niyá ang mésa. (Ramos 1974: 127)
   C$_i$-FN-write-DV 3SG.ng-A SM table
   'He wrote (directly) on the table.'
   b. P-in-ag-sulát-an niyá ang mésa. (Ramos 1974: 127)
   Ci-FN-?-write-DV 3SG.ng-A SM table
   'He wrote on the table./He used the table to write on.'

Ms Danica Salazar, a native speaker of Tagalog, suggests that she is not familiar with this usage.

### 13.1.2. Source

Examples (3b) and (4b) bellow show that the subject NP refers to the source from whom/which something originated.

( 3 ) a. K-um-úha ka ng péra sa kaniyá.
   Ci-AV.IMP-get 2SG.NOM ng-P money from 3SG
   'Get some money from him/her.'

b. Kún-an       mo       siyá      ng   péra.
get-IMP.DV 2SG.ng-A 3SG.NOM ng-P money
'Get some money from him/her'
(NB: *Kúnan* is the irregular form derived from *kúha* + *han*.)

(4) a. Akó        ang mag-a-alís     ng    butó' sa    átis.
                                          (English 1986: 37)
1SG.NOM SM AV-NB-remove np-P seed from custard.apple
'I will take out seeds of the custard apple.'
b. In-alis-án      ng   babáe  ng   pagkáin ang anák.   (BT: 95)
FN-remove-DV ng-A woman ng-P food     SM child
'The woman removed food from her child.'

Note that in (4b), ng-forms appear sequentially (i.e. *ng babáe ng pagkáin*), where the former is A and the latter P. This indicates that ng-A usually comes after the initial verb.

### 13.1.3. Directional

The Directional role is functionally equivalent to the *to-NP* phrase in English. The following are examples of directional voiced sentences.

(5) a. P-um-untá     si   Nóri kay Jóyce.
Ci-AV.FN-go SM Nori to  Joyce
'Nori went to Joyce.'
b. P-in-unta-hán ni           Nóri si  Jóyce sa  báhay.
C$_i$-FN-go-DV PN.SG.ng-A Nori SM Joyce to house
'Nori visited Joyce in her house.'

(6) a. P-um-untá      akó         sa Maynílaʼ noóng   isá-ng   taón.
       Ci-AV.FN-go 1SG.NOM to Manila  when.LK one-LK year
       'I went to Manila last year.'
   b. P-in-unta-hán   ko         ang Maynílaʼ.
       C$_i$-FN-go-DV 1SG.ng-A SM Manila
       'I went to Manila.'
   c. P-in-unta-hán   ko         si   John sa Maynílaʼ.
       C$_i$-FN-go-DV 1SG.ng-A SM John in Manila
       'I visited John in Manila.'

(7) Iláng            lugár ang p-in-unta-hán mo?
    how many.LK place SM C$_i$-FN-go-DV 2SG.ng-A
    'How many places (cities, etc.) did you visit?'

### 13.1.4. Recipient/Benefactive

The (b) sentences below indicate that the subject NPs play a recipient role.

(8) a. Mag-bása         ka          ng        kuwénto sa akin.           (BT: 93)
       AV.IMP-read 2SG.NOM ng-P story     to 1SG
       'Please read a story to me.'
   b. Basá-han         mo          akó        ng        kuwénto.            (BT: 93)
       read-IMP.DV 2SG.ng-A 1SG.NOM ng-P story
       'Please read me a story.'

(9) a. Nag-bigáy       siyá         ng        libró kay Mary.
       AV.FN-give 3SG.NOM ng-P book to Mary
       'S/he gave a book to Mary.'
   b. B-in-igy-án     niyá          ng        libró si Mary.
                                                             (b-in-igy-án < b-in-igay-án)

$C_i$-FN-give-DV  3SG.ng-A  ng-P  book  SM  Mary
'S/he gave Mary a book.'

(10) a. Su-súlat      ako         sa  áking           iná.
     AV.NB-write  1SG.NOM  to  1SG.GEN.LK  mother
     'I will write to my mother.'

   b. Su-sulát-an       ko           ang  áking           iná.
     NB-write-DV  1SG.ng-A  SM   1SG.GEN.LK  mother
     'I will write to my mother.'

(11) a. Mag-báyad   ka          ng    iyó-ng              útang  sa  ákin.
     AV.IMP-pay  2SG.NOM  ng-P  2SG.GEN.LK  debt    to  1SG
     'Pay your debt to me.'

   b. Bayár-an         mo           akó          ng    iyó-ng              útang.
                                                                                              (BT: 95)
     pay-IMP.DV  2SG.ng-A  1SG.NOM  ng-P  2SG.GEN.LK  debt
     'Pay your debt to me.'                                  (bayár-an < bayád-an)

## 13.1.5. A note on the preposition *sa*

I glossed the preposition *sa* as 'to' in (5) through (11), with the exception of (6c). However, *sa* has several meanings along the Directional/Recipient/Benefactive continuum, which will be discussed in Chapter 21.

Interestingly enough, the preposition *sa* has opposite meanings like 'to' and 'from'. Note, however, that this ambiguity does not lead to misunderstanding, because semantic information on the collocation of 'to' and 'from' with verbs like 'to sell' and 'to buy' serves to describe the transaction properly. These verbs clarify *to* which the action is directed or *from* which the action starts.

We shall now consider the following example, which involves another ambiguity.

(12) B-in-il-hán      ko        siyá        ng    manggá.
                                                    (binilhán < b-in-ili-hán)
C$_i$-FN-buy-DV  1SG.ng-A  3SG.NOM  ng-P  mango
'I bought mangoes from him/her.'
'I bought mangoes for him/her.'

Example (12) is ambiguous, as its corresponding AV constructions indicate. See the examples in (13) below.

(13) a. B-um-ilí      akó        ng    manggá *sa*    kaniyá.
      C$_i$-AV.FN-*buy*  1SG.NOM  ng-P  mango  *from*  3SG
      'I bought mangoes from him/her.'
  b. B-um-ilí      akó        ng    manggá *pára sa* kaniyá.
      C$_i$-AV.FN-buy  1SG.NOM  ng-P  mango  *for*     3SG
      'I bought mangoes for him/her.'

It is clear from (13a) and (13b) that *siyá* in (12) has the meanings of both source and benefactive. Note that the ambiguity of (12) results from an optional deletion of the initial prefix *i-* on the verb *bilhán*. Thus, a more accurate example like (14) is not ambiguous.

(14) I-b-in-il-hán        ko        siyá        ng    manggá.
    BEN-C$_i$-FN-buy-DV  1SG.ng-A  3SG.NOM  ng-P  mango
    'I bought mangoes for her/him.'

Although collocation and contextual information disambiguate the source or goal interpretation of the preposition *sa*, it is true that (15) below is still ambiguous (Ramos 1974: 5). Ms Danica Salazar suggested that the preposition *mula'* disambiguates (15a) (p.c., Oct. 17, 2011).

(15) a. Na-húlog    siyá       sa      mésa.           (Ramos 1974: 5)
       AV.FN-fall  3SG.NOM    on/from  table
       'He fell on the table.'    (Goal)
       'He fell from the table.'  (Source)
    b. Na-húlog    siyá       mulá' sa mésa.          (Ms Danica Salazar)
       AV.FN-fall  3SG.NOM    from     table
       'He fell from the table.'  (Source)

## 13.2. Special use of -(h)an verbs: Patient

There are examples in which the affix *-(h)an* is used for semantically PV constructions. Nevertheless, we call them DV constructions, since our analysis is based on morphology. The (b) sentences in (16) through (18) are examples of DV constructions whose subjects represent a patient.

(16) a. Mag-bukás     ka           ng     pintó'.                  (BT: 93)
       AV.IMP-open   2SG.NOM      ng-P   door
       'Open a door.'
    b. Buks-án       mo           ang pintó'. (buks-án < bukas-án) (BT: 93)
       open-IMP.DV   2SG.ng-A     SM  door
       'Open the door.'

(17) a. Nag-labá      ang katúlong ko         ng     áming
       AV.FN-wash    SM  helper   1SG.GEN    ng-P   1PL.EXCL.GEN.LK
       damít.
       cloth
       'My helper washed our (EXCL) clothes.'

b. Ni-lab-hán     ng       katúlong ko          ang áming
   FN-wash-DV  ng-A   helper    1SG.GEN  SM 1PL.EXCL.GEN.LK
   damít.
   cloth
   'My helper washed our clothes.' (ni-lab-hán < ni-laba-hán < l-in-aba-hán)

(18) a. H-um-alík       ang báta' sa kamáy ng       kaniyá-ng
       C¡-AV.FN-kiss SM child on hand      GEN 3SG.GEN-LK
       lóla.
       grandmother
       'The child kissed his/her grandmother on the hand.'
    b. H-in-alik-án      ng    báta' ang kamáy ng      kaniyá-ng
       C¡-FN-kiss-DV ng-A child SM hand       GEN 3SG.GEN-LK
       lóla.                                                     (BT: 95)
       grandmother
       'The child kissed his/her grandmother on the hand.'

It seems that *ang*-marked NPs which are semantically patients of *-(h)an* verbs share certain semantic features: the objects are flat, spread, bounded, etc.

## 13.3.  Conjugation pattern of -(h)an verbs

Table 13–1 below will show the conjugation and accentuation of *-(h)an* verbs. Note that the suffix *-(h)an* and the infix *-in-* are not in complementation, in contrast to the conjugation of *-(h)in* verbs.

Table 13–1: Conjugation pattern of *-(h)an* verbs

| Root Word | alís 'to remove' | súlat 'to write' | labá 'to wash' | Gloss |
|---|---|---|---|---|
| Neutral | alis-án | sulát-an | lab-hán | RW-NT.DV |
| Imperative | alis-án | sulát-an | lab-hán | RW-IMP.DV |
| Perfective | in-alis-án | s-in-ulát-an | ni-lab-hán | (Ci-)FN-RW-DV |
| Imperfective | in-á-alis-án | s-in-ú-sulát-an | ni-lá-lab-hán | (Ci-)BG-UF-RW-DV |
| Inceptive | á-alis-án | sú-sulát-an | lá-lab-hán | NB-RW-DV |

## 13.4. Additional notes on the conjugation pattern of -(h)an verbs

Additional notes are necessary to gain a deeper understanding of the conjugation of *-(h)an* verbs (cf. also Aspillera 1969).

(19) a. When *-(h)an* is suffixed to a root word, the stress of the root word shifts to the next syllable.
 b. When a RW begins with *l*, *w* and *y*, the prefix *ni-*, instead of the infix *-in-*, is used to form the perfective and imperfective forms.
 c. Some RWs delete the vowel of the root-final syllable when *-(h)an* is suffixed: *labá* 'to wash', *lagáy* 'to put', *bigáy* 'to give', *takíp* 'to cover', *dalá* 'to bring', etc.
 d. When a RW ends in a vowel, *h* is inserted between the RW and the suffix *-an*, as in *puntahan*. In the framework of generative phonology, *puntah* is assumed as its underlying representation, with the result that all RWs end in a consonant. It is not plausible to assume that each RW deletes the final *-h* when it does not take the suffix: e.g. /mag-labáh/ → mag-labá. This has already been discussed in the preceding chapter.

## 13.5. Accentuation of -(h)an verbs

The accentuation of *-(h)an* verbs can be described by the following rules, which are basically the same as applied to the *-(h)in* verbs.

(20) a. S$_2$Ś$_1$ + (h)an# → (RÉD)S$_2$S$_1$ + (h)án#
 b. Ś$_2$S$_1$ + (h)an# → (RÉD)S$_2$Ś$_1$ + (h)an#

It thus follows that RED involves the initial (C)V of RWs.

# Chapter 14

# The accusative/ergative controversy

## 14.1. Introduction

So far we have discussed the agent-voiced (AV), patient-voiced (PV) and directional voiced (DV) constructions. This chapter deals with these constructions from the viewpoint of accusative and ergative morphology. As mentioned in Chapters 1 and 3, Tagalog has both accusative and ergative properties. This morphological duality comes from the fact that the language has a multi-voiced system. In addition, the morphological duality has to do with the fact that AV constructions take *indefinite* patient NPs marked with *ng* [naŋ], whereas PV constructions take *definite* patient NPs marked with *ang* [aŋ].

## 14.2. Accusative and ergative morphology

Let us take a brief look at 'morphological ergativity' and 'morphological accusativity'.

Ergative languages treat S and P alike, while accusative languages treat S and A alike, when sentences consist of S, A and P, to the exclusion of V. Thus, a language that shows *S-a V* (intransitive sentence) and *A-b P-a V* (transitive sentence) is morphologically ergative. A language that shows *S-a V* and *A-a P-b V* is morphologically accusative. Note that *S, A* and *P* are NPs while *a* and *b* are case markers. In ergative languages, *a* is the **absolutive** (ABS) case and *b* is the **ergative** (ERG) case. In accusative language, *a* is the nominative case (NOM) and *b* is the **accusative** case (ACC).

Tagalog has both accusative and ergative properties. Examples (1) and (2) support accusative morphology, where Table 14–1 obtains.

(1) P-um-untá    *ang*    mga báta'   sa   eskuwelahán.
     $C_i$-AV.FN-go   NOM   PL    child   to   school
     'The children went to school.'

(2) B-um-ása    ***ng***    mga libró   *ang*    mga báta'.
     $C_i$-AV.FN-read   ACC   PL    book   NOM   PL    child
     'The children read books.'

Table 14–1: Accusative morphology

| V | S<br>ang (NOM) | |
|---|---|---|
| V | A<br>ang (NOM) | **P**<br>**ng (ACC)** |

Examples (3) and (4), on the other hand, reveal ergative morphology, where Table 14–2 obtains.

(3) T-um-akbó    *ang*   mga báta'.
     $C_i$-AV.FN-run   ABS   PL    child
     'The children ran.'

( 4 )  B-in-ása      *ng*    mga báta' *ang*   mga libró.
       Ci-PV.FN-read  ERG    PL   child  ABS   PL  book
       'The children read the book.'

Table 14–2: Ergative morphology

| V | S<br>ang (ABS) |  |
|---|---|---|
| V | A<br>**ng (ERG)** | P<br>ang (ABS) |

## 14.3. Problems with the ergative analysis

There are some problems with the ergative treatment of Tagalog. These problems are (i) how to treat the non-subject **patient** marker **ng** and the directional marker **sa**, (ii) how to treat two types of **ng** (i.e. *ng*-agent and *ng*-patient) and (iii) how to process intransitive Directional voiced (DV) constructions. In this section, we shall examine these problems in that order.

### 14.3.1. How to treat the non-subject patient marker *ng* and the directional marker *sa*

Some linguists (e.g. Payne 1982, Guzman 1988, etc.) label the particle *ng* that marks a non-subject agent as the ergative case marker, and maintain that Tagalog is morphologically ergative (see Table 14–2 above). Instead, they call the transitive AV construction the **anti-passive**. See examples (3) and (4) above, where I used the terms AV and PV, although ergative analysts in fact do not use the terms AV and PV. Admittedly, -*in*- and -*um*- in example (5) below seem to mark ergative and anti-passive constructions, respectively. However, what is important here is that verbal affixes in Tagalog serve not to produce ergative and anti-passive constructions, but to produce voice variations.

(5) a. B-in-ása    ng    propésor ang libró.        (Siewierska 1991: 91)
       Ci-FN-read **ERG** professor **ABS** book
       'The professor read the book.'
   b. B-um-ása    ng    libró ang propésor.        (Siewierska 1991: 91)
       Ci-FN-read **OBL** book **ABS** professor
       'The professor read a book.'

(6) a. B-in-il-hán    ng    báta' ng    libró ang tindáhan.
                                                    (b-in-il-hán < b-in-ili-hán)
       Ci-FN-buy-DV **ERG** child **OBL** book **ABS** store
       'The child bought a book at the store.'
   b. B-um-ilí    ng    libró ang báta' sa    tindáhan.
       Ci-FN-buy **OBL** book **ABS** child **OBL** store
       'The child bought a book at the store.'

Note that in (6a) the particle *ng* appears twice; one is ergative and another oblique. This poses a serious problem for the treatment of the agent NP and the patient NP in non-AV constructions, where the *ng*-marked patient form (i.e. ng-P) is treated as **oblique** (i.e. peripheral), together with the *sa*-marked directional form (see (5) above, Nolasco 2005).

In sum, Table 14–3 below shows case markers from the ergative perspective.

Table 14–3: Ergative treatment of case markers

| | |
|---|---|
| *ang* | absolutive |
| *ng (ng-A)* | ergative |
| *ng (ng-P)* | oblique |
| *sa* | oblique |

It is implausible to treat the ng-P form in ergative constructions like (6a) as **oblique**, because what defines a language as morphologically ergative or accusative is based on the terms **S, A** and **P** (see Blake 1976: 282). There is no good reason to treat the ng-P form *libró* 'book' in (6a) as **oblique**, because *libró* 'book' in (6a) is, in fact, the term **P**. What is more, it is difficult to treat *tindahan* 'store' in (6a) as **absolutive**, although it is marked with *ang*. It is, in fact, an argument other than S, A and P.

We shall look at various case manifestations that appear in actual sentences within the ergative framework. See Table 14–4 below.

Table 14–4: Ergative analysis and case manifestations

| | | | | | |
|---|---|---|---|---|---|
| Intransitive: | V | S | | other arguments | example (3) |
| | | ang | | | |
| | | ABS | | | |
| AV transitive: | V | A | P | other arguments | example (6b) |
| | | ang | ng | sa | |
| | | ABS | OBL | OBL | |
| PV transitive: | V | A | P | other arguments | example (5a) |
| | | ng-A | ang | | |
| | | ERG | ABS | | |
| Non-AV transitive: | V | A | P | other arguments | example (6a) |
| | | ng-A | ng-P | ang | |
| | | ERG | OBL | ABS | |

## 14.3.2. Two types of *ng*

We have so far discussed the controversy over accusative/ergative morphology. We are now in a good position to examine the question of how to treat the two types of **ng** form. The ergative analysis treats the **ang** form and the agent **ng** form as absolutive and ergative, respectively. Within the ergative framework, the patient *ng* is treated as the oblique case marker, along with the directional *sa*, while the agent *ng* is treated as the ergative case marker. Note, however, that the patient NPs in (2) and (4) (i.e. *libró* 'book') differ in *definiteness*. The *ng*-marked patient in (2) is indefinite, while *ang*-marked patient in (4) is definite. Thus, if a patient is definite, the PV construction manifests itself, where the *ang*-marked patient NP serves as the subject. This means that AV constructions cannot express 'I saw *him*', 'John read *the book* yesterday' and the like, because *him* and *the book* are definite, which suggests that the two **ng** forms in (6a) should be clearly distinguished. In order to keep neutral between the accusative and the ergative analysis, we substitute **ng-A** and **ng-P** for the **agent ng** and the **patient ng**, respectively.

### 14.3.3. Intransitive DV constructions

It is interesting to note that Tagalog has a sort of intransitive directional-voiced (DV) construction, as seen in (7c).

( 7 ) a. P-um-untá     akó           sa Maynílaʼ.
       Ci-AV.FN-go  1SG.NOM   to Manila.
       'I went to Manila.'
    b. P-in-unta-hán   ko            ang Maynílaʼ.
       Ci-FN-go-DV  1SG.ng-A   SM  Manila
       'I went to Manila.'
    c. P-in-unta-hán   ko            si   María sa Maynílaʼ.
       Ci-FN-go-DV  1SG.ng-A   SM  Maria  in  Manila
       'I went to Maria in Manila.'

It may be assumed that ergative analysts gloss (7b) and (7c) as follows:

( 8 ) b. P-in-unta-hán  ko            ang   Maynílaʼ. (= (7b))

Ci-FN-go-?   1SG.ERG ABS Manila
'I went to Manila.'

c. P-in-unta-hán ko      si   María sa    Maynílaʼ. (= (7c))
   Ci-FN-go-?   1SG.ERG ABS Maria OBL Manila
   'I went to Maria in Manila.'

It seems that examples (7b) and (7c) above are counter-examples against the ergative analysis, because (7a) that corresponds to (7b) can be regarded as an intransitive sentence, rather than as an anti-passive sentence. Another problem is that it is not clear what gloss ergative analysts would give to the verbal suffix **-han** and how they would analyze the two NPs, *ang Maynílaʼ* in (7b) and *si María* in (7c). Evidently, they are not patient NPs, because they are expressed by *sa Maynílaʼ* and *kay María* in the corresponding AV constructions.

## 14.4. Conclusion

Overall, it is most plausible to assume that Tagalog is **a multi-voiced language**, which correctly explains the morphological duality discussed so far. Voice variations, in fact, come from this multi-voicedness. It must be emphasized that the multi-voiced system is characteristic of Philippine languages. See also Foley (2008), where the term *symmetrical voice* is used instead of the term *multi-voiced* proposed here.

## Chapter 15

## Benefactive/Patient/Instrumental voice: *i*- verbs

## 15.1. Introduction

The aim of this chapter is to make clear the functions of *i*-verbs. It is rather difficult to specify what voice the prefix *i*- represents, because the prefix *i*- has various functions. As mentioned earlier, our classification of verb forms is based on morphology, rather than on semantics. Thus, we referred to verb forms dealt with thus far as *-um-* verbs, *mag-* verbs, *-(h)in* verbs and *-(h)an* verbs. By the same token, we refer to verb forms marked with the prefix *i*- as ***i*- verbs**. It seems that the benefactive and patient uses of *i*-verbs are rule-governed, but the instrumental use is somewhat difficult to specify. In the following section, we will use the terms BV, PV and IV to describe its functions. It goes without saying that the constructions with *i*- verbs are in the non-agent voice.

## 15.2. Benefactive

### 15.2.1. i- verbs: related to root words affixed by -um-

The benefactive use of the prefix *i*- is predictable in that it co-occurs with root words that can take the affix *-um-* in AV constructions (Aspillera 1969: 89). See the following examples. It is worth mentioning that in (2b) the *ng-P* form precedes the *ng-A* form, contrary to our expectations.

( 1 ) a. B-um-ilí     ng   isdá' ang babáe   pára sa kaniyá-ng iná.    (BT: 89)
       Ci-AV.FN-buy ng-P fish  SM  woman  for     3SG-LK    mother
       'The woman bought fish for her mother.'
    b. I-b-in-ilí     ng   babáe   ng   isdá' ang kaniyá-ng iná.
                                                                        (BT: 89)
       BV-C$_i$-FN-buy ng-A woman  ng-P fish  SM  3SG-LK    mother
       'The woman bought her mother fish.'

( 2 ) a. B-um-ása     ng   aklát ang guró'   pára kay Joe.   (BT: 89)
       Ci-AV.FN-read ng-P book  SM  teacher for      Joe.
       'The teacher read a book for Joe.'
    b. I-b-in-ása     ng   aklát ng   guró'   si  Joe.       (BT: 89)
       BV-C$_i$-FN-read ng-P book ng-A teacher SM Joe
       'The teacher read a book for Joe.'

### 15.2.2.  ipag- verbs: related to root words affixed by mag-

When root words take *mag-* in AV constructions, the prefix *ipag-* is used instead of *i-* to form a BV construction. In other words, *mag-* is replaced by *pag-*, to which the prefix *i-* is attached. See below.

( 3 ) a. Mag-labá       ka          ng   damít pára sa  maysakít.
       AV.IMP-wash   2SG.NOM  ng-P cloth for      sick person
       'Please wash clothes for the sick person.'
    b. Ipag-labá      mo         ang maysakít    ng   damít.    (MT: 58)
       BV.IMP-wash  2SG.ng-A SM  sick person ng-P cloth

'Please wash clothes for the sick person.'

## 15.3. Patient: related to root words affixed by mag-

When the prefix *i-* is added to root words that can take *mag-* in an AV construction, the resulting sentences may be patient-voiced (Aspillera 1969: 89). This indicates that to form PV constructions, some root words take *i-* as well as *-(h)in*. See examples (4b), (5b) and (7b), which are all in the PV.

( 4 ) a. Nag-lúto'  siyá  ng  pagkáin pára sa anák.  (BT: 89)
AV.FN-cook 3SG.NOM ng-P food for son/daughter
'S/he cooked food for her/his child.'

b. I-ni-lúto'  niyá  ang pagkáin pára sa anák.  (BT: 89)
PV-FN-cook 3SG.ng-A SM food for son/daughter
'S/he cooked the food for her/his child.'

c. Ni-lúto'  niya  ang pagkáin pára sa anák.
PV.FN-cook 3SG.ng-A SM food for son/daughter
'S/he cooked the food for her/his child.'

( 5 ) a. Nag-bigáy  siyá  ng  péra  sa ákin.
AV.FN-give 3SG.NOM ng-P money to 1SG
'S/he gave some money to me.'

b. I-b-in-igáy  niyá  ang péra  sa ákin.
PV-C$_i$-FN-give 3SG.ng-A SM money to 1SG
'S/he gave the money to me.'

c. B-in-igy-án  niyá  akó  ng  péra.
Ci-FN-give-DV 3SG.ng-A 1SG.NOM ng-P money
'S/he gave me some money.'

(6) a. I-bigáy      mo        ito       sa  kaniyá.
                                              (Constantino 1971: 139)
   PV.IMP-give  2SG.ng-A  this.NOM  to  3SG
   'Please give this to him/her.'
   b. *Big(a)y-ín   mo        ito       sa  kaniyá.
      give-IMP.PV  2SG.ng-A  this.NOM  to  3SG
      'Please give it to me.'

(7) a. Sulát-in       mo       (nga')  ang  kuwénto  pára sa  mga báta'.
       write-IMP.PV  2SG.ng-A  (POL)   SM   story    for     PL   child
       'Please write the story for (the) children.'
   b. I-súlat         mo       (nga')  ang  kuwénto.           (MT: 55)
      PV.IMP-write  2SG.ng-A  (POL)   SM   story
      'Please write the story.'

As is clear from the examples in (7a) and (7b) above, some of the PV sentences can be formed by both *i-* verbs and *(h)in-* verbs, when the question arises of what semantic differences exist between them. (6b) shows that the imperative form of *big(a)y-ín* does not exist; this suggests that which root words can take which affixes is lexically conditioned, which leads us to the assumption that Tagalog has two kinds of PV construction. For the list of root words and affixes that can be attached to them, see Aspillera (1969: 161-177) and Caste and McGonnell (2000: 334-344). One native speaker suggested that (7a) and (7b) differ in politeness, indicating that (7b) is more polite and formal than (7a). It is assumed that *i-sulat* is related to *mag-sulat*, which means 'to write much; to write continuously or repeatedly' (English 1986: 1274).

What has been discussed in Sections 15.2 and 15.3 can be summarized in the following table.

Table 15–1: Use of *i-* verbs and *ipag-* verbs

| Affixes | i- Verbs | ipag- Verbs |
|---------|----------|-------------|
| -um-    | BEN      | —           |
| mag-    | PAT      | BEN         |

## 15.4. Instrumental

Ramos and Cena (1990: 59) indicate that the instrumental prefix is originally *ipang-*, which is usually shortened to *i-*. See the following examples.

(8) a. H-um-íwa'      ka        ng    manggá sa pamamagítan ng
       Ci-AV.IMP-cut 2SG.NOM ng-P mango  by means        GEN
       kutsílyo.
       knife
       'Please cut a mango with the knife.'
    b. Ipang-híwa' mo          ang kutsílyo ng    manggá.      (MT: 59)
       IV.IMP-cut 2SG.ng-A SM knife        ng-P mango
       'Please cut a mango with the knife.'

(9) a. P-um-útol        ka        ng    káhoy sa pamamagítan nitó.
       Ci-AV.IMP-cut 2SG.NOM ng-P wood   by means        this.GEN
       'Please cut wood with this.'
    b. I-pútol       mo       itó        ng    káhoy.
                                                          (Constantino 1971: 139)
       IV.IMP-cut 2SG.ng-A this.NOM ng-P wood
       'Please cut wood with this.'
       (NB: *Ipangputol* can also be used here. (Ms Danica Salazar, p.c.))

## 15.5. Conjugation pattern

The perfective and imperfective forms of root words beginning with vowels, *h*, *l*, *w* and *y*, are realized as *i-ni-(RED)Vst*. The first (C)V of root words is reduplicated in the imperfective and inceptive forms. Note that in Table 15–2, the prefix *i-* itself is used to gloss its functions, for the sake of convenience.

Table 15–2: Conjugation pattern of *i-* verbs

| Root Word | hánap 'to seek' | bilí 'to buy' | túro' 'to teach' | Gloss |
|---|---|---|---|---|
| Neutral | i-hánap | i-bilí | i-túro' | i.NT-RW |
| Imperative | i-hánap | i-bilí | i-túro' | i.IMP-RW |
| Perfective | i-ni-hánap | i-b-in-ilí | i-t-in-úro' | i-(Ci-)FN-RW |
| Imperfective | i-ni-ha-hánap | i-b-in-í-bilí | i-t-in-u-túro' | i-(Ci-)BG-UF-RW |
| Inceptive | i-ha-hánap | i-bí-bilí | i-tu-túro' | i-NB-RW |

## 15.6. Accentuation of i- verbs

It is clear from Table 15–2 that the following rules apply to the accentuation of *i-* verbs.

(10) a. $S_2 \acute{S}_1 \# \rightarrow$ (RÉD) $S_2 \acute{S}_1 \#$
   b. $\acute{S}_2 S_1 \# \rightarrow$ Vacant

# Chapter 16

# The prefix *ma-*

## 16.1. Introduction

The prefix *ma-* has various functions, as seen in Table 16-1 below. Here I notate the different functions with subscript numbers. For more information on this, see Hirano (2007).

Table 16-1: Functions of the prefix *ma-*

|         | Parts of speech    | ±Voluntary | Voice | Examples | Meaning       |
|---------|--------------------|------------|-------|----------|---------------|
| $ma_1$- | Adjective          | —          | —     | *magandá*  | beautiful     |
| $ma_2$- | Intransitive Verb  | +Voluntary | AV    | *malígo'*  | to bathe      |
| $ma_3$- | Intransitive Verb  | −Voluntary | AV    | *magútom*  | to get hungry |
| $ma_4$- | Intransitive Verb  | ±Voluntary | AV    | *mamatáy*  | to die        |
| $ma_5$- | Transitive Verb    | +Voluntary | AV    | *manoód*   | to watch      |
| $ma_6$- | Transitive Verb    | −Voluntary | PV    | *makíta*   | to see        |
| $ma_7$- | (In)transitive Verb| −Voluntary | PV    | *mapútol*  | to break      |

Note that we regard Actor in Foley and Van Valin's (1984) sense as Agent. In what follows, we shall examine each *ma-* prefix in turn.

## 16.2. Adjectival *ma₁-*

Readers may have noticed that *ma-* derives adjectives from RWs. Note that while the verbal prefix *ma-* conjugates, the adjectival prefix *ma-* does not. In this section, we illustrate some examples of sentences in which adjectival *ma-* appears. Incidentally, some adjectives can be formed without the prefix *ma-*, because the RWs themselves can be adjectives, as shown in examples (3)–(5).

(1) Ma-gandá ang bulaklák na itó.
 ADJ-beauty SM flower LK this
 'This flower is beautiful.'

(2) Ma-talíno ang mga estudyánte-ng d-um-a-dálo sa
 ADJ-wise SM PL student-LK $C_i$-AV-UF-attend in
 áking kláse.
 1SG.GEN.LK class
 'The students attending my class are intelligent.'

(3) Báta' pa si Nóri.
 young still SM Nori
 'Nori is still young.' or 'Nori is still a child.'

(4) Sáyang! Tamád na tamád ang mga estudyánte sa Hapón.
 what-a-pity lazy LK lazy SM PL student in Japan
 'Unfortunately, many students in Japan are quite lazy.'

(5) Tahímik ang lugár na itó.
 quiet SM place LK this
 'This place is quiet.'

## 16.3. $ma_2$-: unergative, voluntary

Unergative verbs (UE) denote controllable actions, as seen below.

(6) Ma-li-lígo'     táyo            sa Lagúna.
    AV-NB-bathe  1PL.INCL.NOM  in  Laguna
    'Let us take a bath in Lake Laguna.'

(7) Na-túlog        ang púsa' sa mésa.
    AV-FN-sleep  SM  cat    on table
    'The cat slept on the table.'

(8) Gustó ko-ng           ma-túlog      nang   ma-ága.
    like  1SG.ng-A-LK  AV.NT-sleep  ADVL  ADJ-early
    'I want to sleep early.'

Note that all these verbs have imperative forms. This is in sharp contrast to unaccusative (UA) verbs dealt with in the following section.

## 16.4. $ma_3$-: unaccusative, involuntary

We consider this type of construction as AV, because the subject represents an experiencer role.

(9) Na-gútom         ang púsa' pagkatápos  makipag-áway.
    AV.FN-hungry  SM  cat    after         AV.NT-quarrel
    'The cat got hungry after having a quarrel.'

(10) Na-ga-gálit    ang asáwa ko      sa   ákin. Hindí' ko
     AV-UF-angry   SM  spouse 1SG.GEN with 1SG  not    1SG.ng-A
     alám         kung anó   ang dahilán.
     PV.UF.know   if   what  SM  reason
     'My wife is angry with me. I don't know why.'

(11) Na-lu-lungkót ang mga estudyánte, kasé    b-um-agsák
     AV-UF-sad    SM  PL  student      because Ci-AV.FN-fail
     silá          sa  exám.
     3PL.NOM       in  exam
     'The students feel sad, because they failed in the exam.'

Unaccusative verbs denote feelings, physical conditions, etc. They express not actions, but events that we cannot control. Therefore, it seems likely that they do not have imperative forms. Other examples of this type are: *matákot* 'to be afraid of', *mahiyá* 'to be ashamed of', *maúhaw* 'to become thirsty', etc.

## 16.5.  *ma₄-*: (in)voluntary

Although verbs like 'to die' and 'to fall' denote involuntary events, they can occur with an adverb like *deliberately*, which means that the actions are sometimes done on purpose. This assumes that the prefix ***ma₄-*** must be distinguished from the prefix ***ma₃-***. See the following examples.

(12) Táyo-ng              lahát ay  ma-ma-matáy.  (English: 1977: 257)
     1PL.INCL.NOM-LK      all   TM  AV-NB-die
     'We shall all die.'

(13) Na-húlog    siyá          mulá' sa bubóng.          (English 1986: 664)
    AV.FN-fall  3SG.NOM       from     roof
    'S/he fell from the roof.'

## 16.6.  *ma₅*-: transitive verbs (voluntary action)

Sentences with *ma₅*- verbs denote a voluntary action. They are agent-voiced.

(14) Ma-kiníg       táyo-ng              mabúti  sa títser.
    AV.IMP-listen  1PL.INCL.NOM-LK     good     to teacher.
    'Let us listen to the teacher carefully.'

(15) Ma-no-noód    kamí             ng    síne    búkas.
    AV-NB-watch   1PL.EXCL.NOM    ng-P  movie   tomorrow
    'We are going to watch a movie tomorrow.'

(16) Na-milí      silá          ng    mga gúlay       sa Rustan.
                                                      (mamili < maN-bili)
    AV.FN-buy   3PL.NOM      ng-P   PL  vegetable   in Rustan.
    'They bought vegetables in Rustan.' (Rustan: the name of a supermarket near UP, Diliman)

(17) Ma-ni-niwála'   lang  akó          kung ma-ki-kíta   ko          talagá
    AV-NB-believe  only  1SG.NOM     if    PV-NB-see    1SG.ng-A   true
    ang   multó.
    SM    ghost
    'I will believe in ghosts only if I really see one.'  (maniwála' < maN-tiwála')

## 16.7. $ma_6$- : transitive (involuntary event)

While the prefix $ma_5$- in the previous section is agent-voiced, the prefix $ma_6$- dealt with here is patient-voiced. This is clear from the fact that the sentences with the $ma_6$- verb forms have agents marked with **ng-A**. In addition, the events expressed are all involuntary.

(18) Na-kíta    ng    babáe    ang máma    sa tindáhan.
     PV.FN-see ng-A woman SM mother in store
     'The girl saw her mother in the store.'

(19) Na-i-intindi-hán           ko           kung bákit hindí' ka
     PV-UF-understand-DV 1SG.ng-A if        why   not    2SG.NOM
     t-um-a-táwa.
     C$_i$-AV-UF-laugh
     'I understand why you don't laugh.'

(20) Na-limút-an          ng    babáe    ang wálet niyá        sa sasakyán.
     PV.FN-forget-DV ng-A woman SM wallet 3SG.GEN in vehicle
     'The woman left her wallet in the vehicle.'

*Na-i-intindi-hán* in (19) and *na-limút-an* in (20) are semantically patient-voiced. But we treat them as DV, based on morphology.

## 16.8. $ma_7$-: intransitive/transitive (involuntary action)

$Ma_7$- denotes an involuntary event that has an effect on an object or patient, which are often referred to as 'affectedness'. In $ma_6$- above, such an effect cannot be observed. The following are illustrative sentences in which $ma_7$- verbs are involved.

(21) a. Na-pútol      ang lúbid.
        PV.FN-break  SM rope
        'The rope broke spontaneously.'
    b. Na-pútol      ni          Gári ang lúbid.
        PV.FN-break  PN.SG.ng-A  Gari SM rope
        'Gari broke the rope by accident.'

(22) a. Na-sirá'     ang sílya.
        PV.FN-break  SM chair
        'The chair broke spontaneously.'
    b. Na-sirá'      ni          Vítty ang sílya.
        PV.FN-break  PN.SG.ng-A  Vitty SM chair
        'Vitty broke the chair by accident.'

## 16.9. The prefix *ma-* and morphological ergativity

Observe the following examples.

(23) a. T-um-akbó      ang áso.
        C_i-AV.FN-run  SM dog
        'The dog ran.'
    b. S-um-i-síra'       ng    gátas ang maínit na panahón.
        C_i-AV-UF-spoil   ng-P  milk  SM  hot    LK weather
        'Hot weather spoils milk.'
(24) a. Na_4-matáy  ang áso.
        AV.FN-die   SM dog
        'The dog died.'

b. Na₇-pútol    ni              Gári  ang  lúbid.
   PV.FN-cut  PN.SG.ng-A  Gari  SM   rope
   'Gari broke the rope by accident.'

Note that examples (23a) and (23b) with the infix *-um-* show accusative morphology, while (24a) and (24b) with the prefixes *ma₄-* and *ma₇-*, respectively, manifest ergative morphology.

It is interesting to note that the verb form *s-um-i-síra* 'spoil' in (23b) above expresses spontaneity, although *-um-* verbs usually express voluntary actions. Keep in mind that (23b) is parallel with examples of *-um-* that mean spontaneity like meteorological expressions dealt with in Chapter 26.

# Part III

# Particles

# Chapter 17

# Topic marker: *ay*

## 17.1. Predicate + Subject order

So far, we have dealt with sentences of the type Predicate + Subject, as illustrated in (1) below.

(1) Predicate + Subject order
    a. Estudyánte  siyá.
       student       3SG.NOM
       'S/he is a student.'
    b. Magandá ang mga bulaklák na itó.
       beautiful SM PL flower    LK this
       'These flowers are beautiful.'
    c. T-um-akbó     ang báta'.
       Ci-AV.FN-run SM child
       'The child ran.'
    d. B-um-a-bása      ng   mga libró ang estudyánte sa library.
       $C_i$-AV-UF-read ng-P PL book SM student    in library
       'The student is reading books in the library.'

e. K-in-áin           ng     báta' ang   ságing.
     Ci-PV.FN-eat  ng-A  child  SM    banana
     'The girl ate the banana.'

We referred to these sentences as *situational sentences*.

## 17.2. Subject + ay + Predicate order

Situational sentences can be inverted into the Subject + Predicate order, when the particle *ay* is inserted between the two constituents, where their conceptual meaning does not change. Thus, the particle *ay* has long been called the *inversion marker*.

We shall now turn our attention to the *Subject ay Predicate* order constructions. Note that when *ay* is preceded by words ending in a vowel or the glottal stop, it is often shortened into *y*, where the symbol ' precedes *y*. The examples in (2) are the *ay* versions of the sentences in (1).

( 2 ) Subject + ay + Predicate order
  a. Siyá'y        estudyánte.
     3SG.NOM  student
     'S/he is a student.'
  b. Ang  mga  bulaklák  na   itó  ay  magandá.
     SM   PL   flower    LK   this     beautiful
     'These flowers are beautiful.'
  c. Ang  báta'y  t-um-akbó.
     SM   child   Ci-AV.FN-run
     'The child ran.'
  d. Ang  estudyánte  ay  b-um-a-básá      ng    mga  libró  sa  library.
     SM   student         Ci-AV-UF-read  ng-P  PL   book   in  library

'The student is reading books in the library.'
e. Ang  ságing  ay  k-in-áin         ng      báta'.
   SM   banana     Ci-PV.FN-eat  ng-A  child
   'The girl ate the banana.'

Clearly, the particle *ay* functions to invert Predicate + Subject into Subject + Predicate. However, it is important to note that the particle *ay* also functions to move the subject to initial position, which serves to produce sentential topics. Thus, the particle *ay* is termed *topic marker* (TM), rather than the *inversion marker*. The following section aims to make clear why the particle *ay* can be termed *topic marker* and propose the subject/topic hierarchy.

## 17.3. Sentential topics and the topic marker ay

We are now in a position to examine the function of the TM *ay*. Before proceeding, it must be emphasized that difference in form leads to difference in function. In general, sentence-initial position is of great importance, because it starts a sentence and expresses what the sentence is about. Thus, words or phrases occupying this position have higher topicality and can be called *topics*, when they are often marked by the topic marker or the equivalent. The following are topic constructions in English.

( 3 )  In God   we     trust.
       TOP     SUBJ

( 4 )  As for Nori,  he      is now a linguist.
       TOP          SUBJ

(5) Nora   I like (her) very much.
    TOP  SUBJ

In English, subject and topic often overlap with each other, as seen below.

(6) I    like the Philippines very much.
    TOP/SUBJ

(7) We    trust in God.
    TOP/SUBJ

Needless to say, (3) is derived from (7), where *in God* in (3) is foregrounded as the topic. Their difference lies in *topicality* of the initial elements. Thus, *in God* in (3) is higher in topicality than *we* in (7). Note, however, that the subject has some topicality, as the gloss in (7) shows (for more information on this, see Davison 1984: 809). The notions of topic and subject belong to different components of language structure.

In Tagalog, the particle *ay* serves to denote what the topic is. (1a) illustrates the Predicate + Subject order, and (2a) the Subject + *ay* + Predicate order. Thus, it is clear that the topic *siya* in (2a) is higher in topicality than the subject *siya* in (1a). Data (3)–(7) in English suggest that we should distinguish between two types of topic, the **genuine** topic in (3)–(5) and the subject/topic in (6) and (7). The former is termed '*external topic*' (ET) and the latter '*internal topic*' (IT). With this in mind, compare the sentences in (1) with those in (2). In the sentences in (1), the *ang*-marked NPs and the like serve as ITs, while in the sentences in (2), they serve as ETs and ITs simultaneously. This can be schematized as follows:

(8) a. Predicate   ang NP
                   IT=SUBJ

   b. ang NP        *ay*/Pause  Predicate
     ET=SUBJ/TOP

Schema (8) clearly shows that the *ang*-marked NP preceding the particle *ay* and/or a pause serves as the topic, along with the subject. Now examine sentence (9) below.

(9) Si   Líto  ay   nag-ba-bása  (na)    ng   kómiks.       (IRT: 3)
    SM  Lito  TM  AV-UF-read  (already)  ng-P  comic book
    'Lito is reading a comic book.'

Note that *Lito* in (9) has already been mentioned in discourse, where *Si Lito* functions as an external topic (i.e. TOP) whose grammatical relation is subject (SUBJ).

    For the topical use of *ay*, see also McKaughen (1973) and Hirano (2005).

## 17.4. Adverbial topics

Adverbs of time, place, etc., sometimes precede the TM *ay* and/or a pause, as shown below.

(10) at   doón  ay   na-kíta     nilá     ang isá-ng   Krísto-ng
     and  there  TM  PV.FN-see  3PL.ng-A  SM one-LK  Christ-LK
     na-pa-páko'  sa krus.
     PV-UF-nail  to cross
     '(they went to church), and they saw a Christ nailed to the cross.'
                                                                    (TGA: 20; 20)
     (NB: Native speakers of Tagalog say that *naka-pako'* (STAT-nail) is better than *na-pa-páko'*.)

(11) Sa nobéla-ng itó    ay    s-in-úlat        niyá        ang [...].
     in novel-LK this  TM  Ci-PV.FN-write 3SG.ng-A  SM
     'In this novel, he wrote about [...].'

(12) Sa unáhan nilá,     sa di  kalayúan ay   ma-ta-␣tanáw    ang
     in front 3PL.GEN  in not distance TM  PV-NB-see        SM
     tarangkahán ng    maliít na eskuwelahán.                (TC: 4)
     gate         GEN  small  LK  school
     'Ahead of them, not far away, the gate of a small school will gradually come into view.'

(13) Kung maaári'  ay    i-lípat       ninyó      siyá         sa
     if    possible TM  PV.IMP-move 2PL.ng-A  3SG.NOM   to
     ibá-ng        páaralán.                                  (TC: 4)
     different-LK  school
     'I must ask you to take her to another school, if possible.'

It is clear from examples (10)–(13) that adverbials and the like can be foregrounded as topics when context requires their topicalization.

## 17.5. Subject and topic

### 17.5.1. The connective *ay*

Example (14) below is of interest, because *ang akála' niyá* 'her belief' serves as both subject and topic, and the predicate is a clause that conveys information on 'her belief'.

(14) Ang akála' niyá       ay    si    Red Riding Hood  ang
     SM  belief 3SG.GEN  TM  DET  Red Riding Hood  SM

k-um-a-katók.　　　　　　　　(Si Red Riding Hood: 14)
C$_i$-AV-UF-knock
'She believed that it was Red Riding Hood who was knocking at the door.'
(NB: *Si Red Riding Hood* is the IC$_1$ in the embedded clause, which is a definite sentence. Thus, *si* is glossed as DET.)

The predicate clause in (14), i.e. *si Red Riding Hood ang k-um-a-katók*, is appositive to the initial *ang*-marked phrase. Thus, the topic marker *ay* functions as a connective by which the topic and the comment are combined. In other words, the particle *ay* in Tagalog resembles the topic marker *wa* in Japanese in that they play a role in combing a topic and a comment.

### 17.5.2. Double-subject constructions

Languages often have a construction called 'double-subject'. Tagalog is no exception.

(15) Sa　　Fuji-film, lági-ng　　magandá ang pícture ko.
　　　　　　　　　　　　　　　　　　　　(from an advertisement)
　　LOC Fuji-film always-LK beautiful SM picture 1SG.GEN
　　'The Fuji film makes my picture always beautiful.'

It is plausible to term (15) a topic-subject construction rather than a double-subject construction, where the initial phrase serves as the topic and the second *ang*-marked phrase as the subject. Examples (14) and (15) above are typical examples of the topic-comment construction, where the comment is autonomous as a clause.

Finally, it is worth mentioning that languages such as Indonesian, Chinese and Japanese have topic-subject constructions, as illustrated below.

(16) 'The elephant is such that it has a long trunk.'
    a. Indonesian: Gajah   itu   panjang  belalai-nya.      (Ushie 1975: 36)
                      elephant the   long     nose-his/its
                      TOP                   SUBJ
    b. Chinese:     Xiàng   bízi  cháng.       (Li and Thompson 1981: 92)
                      elephant nose long
                      TOP     SUBJ
    c. Japanese:    Zoo     wa    hana ga     nagai.
                      elephant TM   nose NOM long
                      TOP         SUBJ

## 17.6. The subject/topic hierarchy

What we have discussed so far suggests that subject and topic must be clearly distinguished. In addition, it turned out that there exists a principled order between a subject and a topic, as seen in (17). This principled order can be referred to as the 'subject/topic hierarchy'.

(17) **Subject/topic hierarchy: Topic first, subject later.**

Finally, I will conclude this chapter by quoting Blake (1994: 141): "In most languages the subject, which typically encodes the topic, precedes the object either as the result of a discourse-pragmatic strategy or a grammatical rule. Rules placing first and second person ahead of third can be interpreted as reflecting a *topic-first* principle (emphasis mine)."

# Chapter 18

# Question marker *ba*

## 18.1. Yes-no questions

Yes-no questions in Tagalog can be formed by inserting the question marker *ba* (Q) between the predicate and the subject, as seen below.

(1) Doktór ba kayó?
    doctor Q 2PL.NOM
    'Are you a doctor?'
    (NB: *Kayo* is the second person plural form, but it is commonly used as an honorific form for a single addressee.)

(2) Abalá ba si Jorge?           (Ramos and Cena 1990: 84)
    busy Q SM George
    'Is George busy?'

(3) S-um-ayáw ba ang babáe kahápon?
    Ci-AV.FN-dance Q SM woman last night
    'Did the woman dance last night?'

(4) B-um-ása      ba si  María ng    libró?
    Ci-AV.FN-read Q  SM  Maria ng-P  book
    'Did Maria read a book?'

(5) K-in-áin         mo         ba ang isdá'?
    Ci-PV.FN-eat 2   SG.ng-A    Q  SM  fish
    'Did you eat the fish?'

Ramos (1971b: 118) indicates that the question marker *ba* usually follows the first **full** word of a sentence (emphasis mine). Seemingly, this constraint excludes (5), where *ba* appears after the mono-syllabic *mo* '2SG.ng-A'. It is necessary, in this section, to make clear what is meant by the first **full** word. Observe the following examples.

(6) a. B-um-ása      ba ng    libró si  María?
       Ci-AV.FN-read Q  ng-P  book SM  Maria
       'Did Maria read a book?'
    b. B-um-ása      ba si  María ng    libró? (= (4))
       Ci-AV.FN-read Q  SM  Maria ng-P  book
       'Did Maria read a book?'
    c. *B-um-ása     ng    libró ba si  María?
       Ci-AV.FN-read ng-P  book  Q  SM  Maria
       'Did Maria read a book?'

Based on the sentences in (6), we can formalize where Q appears.

(7) a.  V   Q   O   S
    b.  V   Q   S   O
    c. *V   O   Q   S

(7) shows that Q appears after V that begins a sentence. Conversely, Q does not appear after a sequence of VO, as shown in (7c). That is, Q must be inserted between the sentence-initial verb and S/O. But if the agent is the second person singular (i.e. *ka* and *mo*), *ba* comes after the pronouns (see example (5)). This is because the forms *ka* and *mo* are mono-syllabic. Thus, it turns out that the first full word of a sentence must be content words such as sentence-initial verbs, predicative nouns and adjectives that consist of more than one syllable. Thus, (7) will be collapsed as follows:

( 8 ) V/N/A  Q   S/O

Formula (8) shows that a correct yes-no question is produced if and only if the question marker Q appears after the predicates that begin a sentence. More specifically, Q is a particle or a clitic that appears in the second position of a yes-no question. To conclude, nouns, adjectives and verbs that begin a sentence are involved in the first full word.

Recall that when pronouns are used for subjects of a situational sentence, the VSO order appears, as in (10a).

( 9 ) a. K-um-áin      ng     manggá  si   Pédro.
         Ci-AV.FN-eat ng-P  mango   SM  Pedro
         'Pedro ate a mango.'
    b. K-um-áin      si   Pédro  ng     manggá.
         Ci-AV.FN-eat SM  Pedro  ng-P  mango
         'Pedro ate a mango.'

(10) a. K-um-áin      siyá       ng    manggá.
         Ci-AV.FN-eat 3SG.NOM  ng-P mango
         'S/he ate a mango.'

b. *K-um-áin      ng     manggá siyá.
   Ci- AV.FN-eat ng-P mango    3SG.NOM
   'S/he ate a mango.'

Finally, the question marker *ba* is not obligatorily used in yes-no questions, because a *rising* intonation indicates that the sentence at issue is a yes-no question.

## 18.2. *Wh*-questions

*Wh*-questions accompanied by a *falling* intonation do not necessarily require the question marker. This is because interrogative words such as *síno* 'who', *anó* 'what', *saán* 'where', etc., denote interrogation. In relation to this, Schachter and Otanes (1972: 424) remark that the question marker is more frequently omitted in *wh*-questions than in yes-no questions. Note that some *wh*-questions may be accompanied by the rising intonation; see (13b) and (14b) below. (11)–(20) below are examples of *wh*-questions with the particle *ba*, with the exception of (13b) and (14b).

(11) Síno ba  kayó?
     who  Q  2PL.NOM
     'Who are you?'

(12) Kanínо ba ang báhay na iyán?                    (BT: 28)
     whose  Q  SM house LK that
     'Whose is that house?'

(13) a. Anó ba ang pangálan mo?
        what Q SM name      2SG.GEN

'What is your name?'
b. Anóng pangálan mo?  < Anó ang pangálan mo?
'What's your name?'
(This is more frequently used.)

(14) a. Ilán      ba  ang anák         mo?
　　　　how.many  Q   SM  son/daughter  2SG.GEN
　　　　'How many children do you have?'
　　 b. Iláng anák mo? < Ilán ang anák mo?
　　　　'How many children do you have?'
　　　　(This is more frequently used.)

(15) a. Saán  ba  kayo       pu-puntá?                    (BT: 31)
　　　　wher  Q   2PL.NOM    AV.NB-go
　　　　'Where are you going?'
　　 b. Saán   ka         pu-puntá?
　　　　where  2SG.NOM    AV.NB-go
　　　　'Where are you (SG) going?'
　　　　(Examples (15a) and (15b) are often used as a kind of greeting.)

(16) Nasaán  ba  si  María?
　　 where   Q   SM  Maria
　　 'Where is Maria?'

It must be noted that *saán* and *nasaán* differ in meaning. *Saán* denotes goal or direction, while *nasaán* denotes stationary location; compare *Saán ka pupuntá?* 'Where are you goig?' and *Nasaán siya?* 'Where is s/he?'.

(17) Kailán ba kayó       d-um-atíng?
    when  Q  2PL.NOM  Ci-AV.FN-arrive
    'When did you arrive?'

(18) Paáno  ka         ba  pu-puntá?
    how   2SG.NOM  Q   AV.NB-go
    'How will you go?'

(19) Bákit  mo         ba  k-in-áin         ang  áking         manggá?
    why  2SG.ng-A  Q   Ci-PV.FN-eat  SM  1SG.GEN.LK  mango
    'Why did you eat my mango?'

(20) Magkáno   ba  itó?
    how.much  Q   this
    'How much is this?'

## 18.3.  Position of the question marker *ba*

### 18.3.1.  The number of syllables: agent pronouns

As mentioned in Section 18.1, the question marker follows the first full word. It must be kept in mind, however, that when monosyllabic words such as *ka* '2SG.NOM' and *mo* '2SG.ng-A' appear, it follows them, partly because the sequence of *ka* + *ba* is more euphonious than that of *ba* + *ka*. We call this constraint the monosyllabic principle.

(21) a. A-alís        ka         ba?
       AV.NB-leave  2SG.NOM  Q
       'Are you going to leave?'

b. A-alís       ba  kayó?
   AV.NB-leave  Q   2PL.NOM'
   'Are you going to leave?'

c. A-alís       ka       na      ba?
   AV.NB-leave  2SG.NOM  already Q
   'Are you going to leave already?'

d. *A-alís      na       ka       ba?
    AV.NB-leave already  2SG.NOM  Q
   'Are you going to leave already?'

(22) a. Kailán  ka       ba  d-um-atíng?
        when    2SG.NOM  Q   Ci-AV.FN-arrive
        'When did you arrive?'

b. Kailán  ba  siyá     d-um-atíng?
   when    Q   3SG.NOM  Ci-AV.FN-arrive
   'When did s/he arrive?'

## 18.3.2. *Wh*-questions and subject pronouns

Keep in mind that in *wh*-questions, pronouns in the nominative case precede predicative verbs, as in (23b), where the first full word principle and the monosyllabic principle for the question marker *ba* still obtain. See the following examples.

(23) a. Bákit  u-uwí'          si   María?
        why    AV.NB-go.home   SM   Maria
        'Why will Maria go home?'

b. Bákit  (ba)  siyá      u-uwí'?
   why    (Q)   3SG.NOM   AV.NB-go.home
   'Why does s/he go home?'

c. Bákit ka      ba u-uwí?
   why  2SG.NOM Q  AV.NB-go.home
   'Why are you going home?'

### 18.3.3. *Ay* sentences and *ba*

As the following examples indicate, the question marker *ba* precedes *ay* in sentences with the topic marker *ay*.

(24) Silá     ba ay estudyánte?
     3PL.NOM  Q  TM student
     'Are they students?'

(25) Ang babáe ba ay mabaít?
     SM  woman Q  TM kind
     'Is the woman kind?'

(26) Silá     ba ay a-alís       búkas?
     3PL.NOM  Q  TM AV.NB-leave  tomorrow
     'Do they leave tomorrow?'

## 18.4. Responses to yes-no questions

Affirmative responses to yes-no questions are formed by placing *oo* 'yes', *óho*' and *ópo*' (getting more polite in that order) before the statement. (27) and (28) below illustrate two pairs of examples with yes-no question and affirmative response, taken from Ramos and Cena (1990: 86).

(27) a. Sundálo ba si         Jorge?
        soldier  Q  PN.SG.NOM George

'Is George a soldier?'
b. Oo, sundálo siyá.
   yes soldier 3SG.NOM
   'Yes, he is a soldier.'

(28) a. Pángit ba ang síne?
       ugly Q SM movie
       'Was the movie lousy?'
    b. Oo, pángit ang síne.
       yes ugly SM movie
       'Yes, the movie was lousy.'

Negative responses to yes-no questions are formed by placing *hindi'* 'no/not' just before the statement. When pronouns are used for the subject, the negation marker precedes them, as in *hindi' siya* + Predicate. See below.

(29) a. Doktór ba si John?
       doctor Q SM John
       'Is John a doctor?'
    b. Hindí', hindí' siyá doktór.
       no not 3SG.NOM doctor
       'No, he is not a doctor.'

(30) a. Masípag ba siyá?
       diligent Q 3SG.NOM
       'Is s/he diligent?'
    b. Hindí', hindí' siyá masípag.
       no not 3SG.NOM diligent
       'No, s/he is not diligent.'

Interestingly enough, *hindi'* in Tagalog is equivalent to *no* and *not* in English or *nein* and *nicht* in German, as indicated by (29b) and (30b) above.

## 18.5. Responses to negative questions

When we agree on a negative comment, *oo* 'yes' is placed just before the statement. This is in marked contrast to English, because English uses *no* whenever hearers agree on a negative statement. Examples (31) and (32) are taken from Ramos and Cena (1990: 86). We call the English type the absolutive response system while we call the Tagalog type the relative response system.

(31) a. Hindí' doktór si  Jorge, ano?
        not    doctor  SM George what
    'George isn't a doctor, is he?'
  b. *Oo, hindí'* siyá         doktór.
     yes  not    3SG.NOM  doctor
    '*No*, he is *not* a doctor?'

(32) a. Hindí' pángit ang  síne,   ano?
        not    ugly   SM   movie  what
    'The movie wasn't lousy, was it?'
  b. *Oo, hindí'* pángit ang    síne.
     yes  not    ugly   NOM   movie
    '*No*, the movie was *not* lousy.'

Note that this use of *oo* 'yes' is quite similar to the use of *hai* 'yes' in Japanese. Japanese is also included in the relative response system.

## 18.6. Positions of the question marker across languages

It is interesting to note that among languages that use a question marker, the position of the marker differs, depending on their basic word order, as seen below.

(33) a. Japanese (SOV): **SOV-Q**

Anata wa kinoo tagarogugo o benkyoo-si-masi-ta ***ka***.
2SG TM yesterday Tagalog ACC study-do-POL-PAST Q
'Did you study Tagalog yesterday?'

b. English (SVO): **Q-SVO**

***Did*** you study Tagalog yesterday?

c. Russian (SVO): **V-Q-S (O)**

Govorite ***li*** by po-anglijski?
speak Q you English

The examples in (33) show that question markers appear in three different positions in a sentence: initial (English), final (Japanese) and medial (Russian). As is clear, the question marker *ba* in Tagalog appears sentence-medially.

To sum up, when the agent NP is a pronoun, the question marker *ba* appears differently according to its syllable number. The following schema shows its distribution.

(34) Tagalog (VSO): **V-S₁-Q-O** or **V-Q-S₂-O** (**S₁**: monosyllabic pronoun, **S₂**: disyllabic pronoun)

a. Nag-áral ka ***ba*** ng Tagálog kahápon?
AV.FN-study 2SG.NOM Q ng-P Tagalog yesterday
'Did you study Tagalog yesterday?'

b. Nag-áral ***ba*** siyá ng Tagálog kahápon?
AV.FN-study Q 3SG.NOM ng-P Tagalog yesterday

'Did s/he study Tagalog yesterday?'

# Chapter 19

# Negation: *hindí'*

## 19.1. Negative sentence formation

Negative sentences are formed by placing the negative marker *hindí'* before the corresponding affirmative sentences. When a pronoun is the subject, the pronoun follows *hindí'*. Regarding the formation of negative sentences, see the following schema.

(1) a. Hindí' PRED     NP: SUBJ
    b. Hindí' PRN: SUBJ PRED

## 19.2. Examples

### 19.2.1. *Hindí'* + PRED + NP: SUBJ

We shall take some examples of the type *Hindí + PRED + NP: SUBJ*.

(2) Hindí' Pilipíno si    Taroo.
    not      Filipino SM Taro
    'Taro is not a Filipino.'

(3) Hindí mabaít si John.
　　 not　 kind　 SM John
　　 'John is not kind.'

(4) Hindí' a-alís　　　 si　 Mary búkas.
　　 not　 AV.NB-leave SM Mary tomorrow
　　 'Mary does not leave tomorrow.'

(5) Hindí' mag-a-áral　　si　 Jack ng　 Ilokáno.
　　 not　 AV-NB-study SM Jack ng-P Ilokano.
　　 'Jack will not study Ilokano.'

### 19.2.2. *Hindí'* + PRN: SUBJ + PRED

In this section, we illustrate examples of the type *Hindí'* + *PRN: SUBJ* + *PRED*.

(6) Hindí' siyá　　　　 Hapón.
　　 not　 3SG.NOM Japanese
　　 'S/he is not Japanese.'

(7) Hindí' akó　　　　 masípag.
　　 not　 1SG.NOM diligent
　　 'I'm not diligent.'

(8) Hindí' silá　　　　 pu-puntá　 sa Pilipínas.
　　 not　 3PL.NOM AV.NB-go to Philippines
　　 'They will not go to the Philippines.'

(9) Hindí' akó　　　　 k-um-áin　　　　ng　　 balót.
　　 not　 1SG.NOM Ci-AV.FN-eat ng-P balot

'I didn't eat a ballot.'
(NB: *Balot* is a boiled duck's egg with partially developed embryo. [TD: 33] notates this as *balút*.)

It must be kept in mind that pronoun subjects occupy a specific position. The examples above indicate that they appear immediately after *hindi'*. The position of pronouns also applies to situational sentences, where pronouns appear after the first full words. Thus, we call this phenomenon the second position principle of pronouns.

## 19.3. Use of *hindí'* in the *ay*-sentences

In sentences with genuine topics marked with *ay*, the negation marker *hindí'* follows *ay*, as seen below.

(10) Si   John  ay    hindí'  gúro'.
     SM John TM    not     teacher
     'John is not a teacher.'

(11) a. Ang  Hapón ay    hindí'  maínit.
       SM   Japan  TM    not     hot
       'It is not hot in Japan.'
   b. Hindí'  maínit sa  Hapón.
      not      hot    in Japan
      'It is not hot in Japan.'
   c. Hindí'  maínit ang  Hapón.
      not      hot    SM   Japan
      'It is not hot in Japan.'

(12) Ang áso   ay    hindí' t-um-ahól       kagabí.
     SM  dog   TM    not    Ci-AV.FN-bark   yesterday
     'The dog didn't bark yesterday.'

(13) (Ang) búhay  ni           Pédro'y   dí'   masayá.
                                    (Aguilar: Kasaysayan ni Pedro)
     (SM)  life   PN.SG.GEN    Pedro TM  not   happy
     'Pedro's life is not happy.'

(14) Siyá        ay    hindí' nag-áral      ng    Inggles  kahápon.
     3SG.NOM     TM    not    AV.FN-study   ng-P  English  yesterday
     'S/he didn't study English yesterday.'

Recall that the sentence initial forms in (10), (11a) and (12)–(14) serve as both subject and topic.

# Chapter 20

# Case marking

## 20.1. Common nouns

Table 20–1 shows the case markers for common nouns.

Table 20–1: Common nouns

| Cases | Singular/(Plural) | Definiteness | ACC or ERG |
|---|---|---|---|
| NOM | ang (mga) N | +definite | NOM: ABS |
| ng-A | ng (mga) N | ±definite | GEN: ERG |
| Dative | sa (mga) N | ±definite | DAT: OBL |
| ng-P | ng (mga) N | −definite | ACC: OBL |

The following are examples in which these case markers are involved.

( 1 ) Estudyánte      ang  laláki
      student (NOM)   SM   man
      'The man is a student.'

(2) Malakí ang báhay ng       laláki.
    big       SM  house GEN man
    'The man's house is big.'

(3) Nag-bigáy    siyá        ng    péra   sa    anák.
    AV.FN-give  3SG.NOM     ng-P  money  DAT   son/daughter
    'S/he gave some money to her/his child(ren).'

(4) a. K-um-áin       ng    manggá ang  báta'.
       Ci-AV.FN-eat  ng-P  mango   SM   child
       'The child ate **a**/*the mango.'
    b. K-in-áin       ng    báta' ang  manggá.
       Ci-PV.FN-eat  ng-A  child  SM   mango
       'The child ate **the**/*a mango.'

As mentioned in Chapter 14, **ng-A** and **ng-P** differ in function, although they are identical in form. As seen in (4b) above, when the patient noun is definite, the PV construction automatically surfaces, because **ng-P** cannot denote a definite referent. Recall that the ergative analysis glosses these two *ng* forms as ergative and oblique, respectively (e.g. Nolasco 2005).

It is worth mentioning that the particle *ang* may be glossed as Ø, because in (1) above, nothing precedes the nominal predicate *estudyante*, when it can be treated as the determiner.

## 20.2. Demonstratives

The demonstratives in Tagalog have the tripartite system: *itó* 'this', *iyán* 'that' and *iyón* 'that yonder'. They denote something or someone near the speaker and the hearer, near the hearer, and far from the speaker and the hearer, respectively. See

Table 20–2 below.

Table 20–2: Demonstratives

| Cases | Singular/Plural | Singular/Plural | Singular/Plural |
|---|---|---|---|
| NOM | itó/ang mga itó | iyán/ang mga iyán | iyón/ang mga iyón |
| ng-A | nitó/ng mga itó | niyán/ng mga iyán | noón/ng mga iyón |
| DAT | díto | diyán [ʤá·n] | doón |
| ng-P | nitó /ng mga itó | niyán/ng mga iyán | noón/ng mga iyón |

Incidentally, Tagalog has the form *iri*, which denotes something in the speaker's hand.

We are now in a position to illustrate various uses of *ito* with examples.

( 5 ) a. Báhay ko      itó.
       house  1SG.GEN  this.NOM
       'This is my house.'
    b. Malakí ang báhay na itó.
       big    SM  house  LK this.NOM
       'This house is big.'
    c. Malakí itó-ng           báhay.
       big    this.NOM-LK     house
       'This house is big.'
    d. Malakí itó-ng        baháy na itó.
       big    this.NOM-LK  house  LK this.NOM
       'This house is big.'

In (5d), *bahay* 'house' is sandwiched between *ito* and *ito*. Note, incidentally, that Kimaragang of Sabah has expressions like *itih tasin ditih* (this-salt-this) 'this salt' (Kroeger 1988, Foley 2008: 29), which implies that this use of *ito* is of Austronesian origin.

In the rest of this section, we show examples in which the *ng-P* form of *ito* is involved.

(6) G-um-awá'      nitó       si María.
    Ci-AV.FN-make  this.ng-P  SM Maria
    'Maria made this.'

Curiously enough, this example shows that the ng-P demonstratives can be used in the AV sentences, despite the fact that they are definite, where this *nito* is in the accusative case. Note that this use of *nito* serves to produce a sentence of the following type. (7b) may also be possible.

(7) a. Síno ang g-um-awá'      nitó?
       who  SM  Ci-AV.FN-make  this.ng-P
       'Who made this?'
    b. G-in-awá'       itó        níno?
       Ci-PV.FN-make   this(NOM)  who.ng-A
       Intended: 'Was it made by whom?'

Finally, *dito* is used to show the place where something/somebody exists or an action occurs. Examples of *dito* are as follows:

(8) a. May libró díto.
       exist book here
       'There is a book here.'
    b. Nag-la-laró'  ang mga báta' díto.
       AV-UF-play   SM  PL  child here
       'The children are playing here.'

## 20.3. Human proper nouns

Human proper nouns have the tripartite case system, as shown in Table 20–3.

Table 20–3: Human proper nouns

| Cases | Singular | Plural |
|---|---|---|
| NOM | si N | siná N |
| ng-A | ni N | niná N |
| DAT | kay N | kiná N |
| ng-P | — | — |

The following examples show how the markers for human proper nouns are used.

(9) Mabaít na  mabaít si  Ría.
    kind  LK kind   SM Ria
    'Ria is very kind.'

(10) a. G-in-awá'        itó         ni            María.
        Ci-PV.FN-make this.NOM PN.SG.ng-A Maria
        'Maria made this.'
     b. G-in-awá'        ni            María itó.
        Ci-PV.FN-make PN.SG.ng-A Maria this.NOM
        'Maria made this.'

(11) Nag-bigáy    siná    Tóny ng  mga manggá kay  Tína.
     AV.FN-give SM.PL Tony ng-P PL  mango   DAT Tina
     'Tony and his friends gave some mangoes to Tina.'

(12) a. Na-kíta      ni              Nóri  si   Tína.
       PV.FN-see  PN.SG.ng-A  Nori  SM  Tina
       'Nori saw Tina.'
   b. *Naka-kíta   si    Nóri  ni              Tína.
       AV.FN-see  SM  Nori  PN.SG.ng-P  Tina
       Intended: 'Nori saw Tina.'

Recall that Tagalog lacks the ng-P marker for definite nouns, with the exception of demonstratives. This also applies to the case marking system of human proper nouns, since they are definite. As mentioned in Section 20.1, when patient NPs are definite, PV constructions automatically manifest themselves. Example (12b) above is not grammatical, due to this constraint. It must be kept in mind, however, that (12b) and related examples are acceptable in **Cebuano**, since it has the ng-P marker for human proper nouns, as shown below (Shibatani 1988: 107).

(13) a. Ni-kumusta   si    Juan  *ni*             Pedro.
       AV.FN-greet  SM  Juan  PN.SG.**ng-P**  Pedro
       'Juan saw Pedro.'
   b. Gi-palit         **sa**       magdadaro  ang  karabao.
       PV.FN-buy  **ng-A**  farmer         SM    buffalo
       'The farmer bought the buffalo.'

Note that in (13), I have used the terms AV and PV instead of AF and GF used by Shibatani (1988).

## 20.4.   Personal pronouns

It is clear from our observations so far that Tagalog does not have the ng-P marker for definite nouns, with the exception of demonstratives. Thus, human proper nouns and personal pronouns equivalent to ng-P forms are absent, because they are all definite. See Table 20–4 below, where ng-A1 and ng-A2 are distinguished. The former represents a preposed ng-A form and the latter a postposed ng-A form. The plural form of *síno* and *kaníno* can be formed by repeating the first two syllables of the singular form, producing *sínu-síno* and *kaní-kaníno*. This process applies to interrogatives in general; *anu-ano* 'what', *ilan-ilan* 'how many', *magka-magkano* 'how much', etc.

Table 20–4: Personal pronouns and the interrogatory *who*

| Person | 1 | | | 2 | | 3 | | 'who' |
|---|---|---|---|---|---|---|---|---|
| Number | SG | PL EXCL | PL INCL | SG | PL | SG | PL | SG |
| NOM | akó | kamí | táyo | ka/ikáw | kayó | siyá | silá | síno |
| ng-A1 | ákin | ámin | átin | iyó | inyó | kaniyá | kanilá | kaníno |
| ng-A2 | ko | námin | nátin | mo | ninyó | niyá | nilá | níno |
| DAT | sa ákin | sa ámin | sa átin | sa iyó | sa inyó | sa kaniyá | sa kanilá | sa kaníno |
| ng-P | — | — | — | — | — | — | — | — |

The following are examples in which personal pronouns are involved.

(14) Tulúng-an        mo              ang iyó-ng         saríli.
                                                          (Aguilar: Anak/Alaala)
     help-IMP.DIR 2SG.ng-A2 SM 2SG.GEN-LK self
     'Please help yourself.'

(15) Nag-túro'      akó         ng    Tagálog sa     kanilá.
     AV.FN-teach 1SG.NOM ng-P Tagalog DAT 3PL
     'I taught Tagalog to them.'

Note that in (14) the ng-A2 form *mo* (Agent) triggers reflexivization (cf.

Schachter 1976, 1977).

It is necessary here to show how *ikáw* (2SG.NOM) is used, because both *ikáw* and *ka* denote 2SG.NOM. Keep in mind that basically *ikáw* stands sentence-initially, otherwise *ka* is used. The two forms are in complementary distribution, as (16a) and (16b) below indicate.

(16) a. Ikáw       ba  ay  estudyánte?
       2SG.NOM  Q   TM  student
       'Are you a student?'
    b. Estudyánte         ka        ba?
       Student (NOM)  2SG.NOM  Q
       'Are you a student?'

(17a) below seems exceptional, but it may be the topicalized version of (17b) in which *ikaw* appears sentence-initially. (17b) can be classified as a definite sentence.

(17) a. Ang  mahál    ko              ikáw. (the title of a Philippine popular song)
       SM   PV.love  1SG.ng-A2  2SG.NOM
       'It's you whom I love.'
    b. Ikáw         ang  mahál    ko.
       2SG.NOM  SM   PV.love  1SG.ng-A2
       'It's you whom I love.'

## 20.5. Further discussion

### 20.5.1. Evidence that Tagalog lacks the *ng-P* form for definite nouns

As mentioned repeatedly, Tagalog lacks the *ng-P* form for definite nouns, with the exception of demonstratives. In embedded clauses, however, definite nouns appear in the dative case, as in (19b).

(18) a.*P-um-atáy     akó         niyá.
       Ci-AV.FN-kill  1SG.NOM     3SG.ng-P
       Intended: 'I killed him/her.'
    b. P-in-atáy      ko          siyá.
       Ci-PV.FN-kill  1SG.ng-A2   3SG.NOM
       'I killed him/her.'

(19) a. Ang   báta'  ang  k-um-áin      **ng**   manggá.
        DET   child  SM   Ci-AF.FN-eat  ng-P     mango
        'It was the child who ate **a** mango.'
     b. Ang   báta'  ang  k-um-áin      **sa**   manggá. (Constantino 1970: 66)
        DET   child  SM   Ci-AF.FN-eat  DAT     mango
        'It was the child who ate **the** mango.'

## 20.5.2. Causative constructions

Causative constructions are of importance in considering case marking. There are two types of causative construction. One is the type whose embedded clause is *intransitive*. Another is the type whose embedded clause is *transitive*. Cross-linguistically, in the former type a subject of the embedded clause is promoted to the object (ACC) or the indirect object (DAT) of the main clause, while in the latter it is promoted to the indirect object (DAT) of the main clause. Thus, it is expected that in Tagalog, the former type of causative construction accepts the *ng*-marked **indefinite** NP as the causee, whereas the latter type of causative construction accepts the DAT NP preceded by **sa** (with personal pronouns) and **kay** (with human proper nouns) as the causee. See the following examples.

***Intransitive clauses embedded:***

(20) a. Mag-pa-pa-takbó **ng** báta' si Títo.
   AV-CAUS-NB-run ng-P child SM Tito
   'Tito will make a/*the child run.'

   b. Mag-pa-pa-iyák si Títo **ng** báta'.
   AV-CAUS-NB-cry SM Tito ng-P child
   'Tito will make a/*the child cry.'

   c. Mag-pa-pa-túlog si Rény **ng** báta'.
   AV-CAUS-NB-sleep SM Reny ng-P child
   'Reny will make a/*the child sleep.'

(21) a. *Mag-pa-pa-takbó si Tóny sa ákin.
   AV-CAUS-NB-run PN.NOM Tony DAT 1SG
   'Tony will make me run.'

   b. *Mag-pa-pa-takbó si Tóny ko.
   AV-CAUS-NB-run PN.NOM Tony 1sg.ng-P
   'Tony will make me run.'

   c. Pa-ta-takbu-hín akó ni Tóny
   CAUS-NB-run-PV 1SG.NOM PN.ng-A Tony
   'Tony will make me run.'

(22) a.*Mag-pa-pa-ka-gálit si Tóny sa ákin.
   AV-CAUS-NB-?-angry PN.NOM Tony DAT 1SG
   'Tony will make me get angry.'

   b. *Mag-pa-pa-ka-gálit si Tóny ko.
   AV-CAUS-NB-?-angry PN.NOM Tony 1SG.ng-P
   'Tony will make me get angry.'

   c. G-in-a-galit ako ni Tony.
   Ci-PV-UF-angry 1SG.NOM PN.ng-A Tony

'Tony is making me angry.'

(21a-b) and (22a-b) show that the AV causative construction with personal pronouns as the causee cannot be accepted. This demonstrates that *ng-P* forms do not exist in the case marking system of personal pronouns, because they are definite.

**Transitive clauses embedded:**
(23) a. Mag-pa-pa-patáy    si  Títo  ng    manók **kay**  Rény.
       AV-CAUS-NB-kill SM Tito ng-P chicken DAT Reny
       'Tito will make Reny kill a chicken.'
    b. Mag-pa-pa-síra'    si  Títo  ng    sílya **kay**  Rény.
       AV-CAUS-NB-break SM Tito ng-P chair DAT Reny
       'Tito will make Reny break a chair.'
    c. Mag-pa-pa-lúto'    si  Títo **kay**  Rény ng    kánin para kay Ría.
       AV-CAUS-NB-cook SM Tito DAT Reny ng-P rice   for    Ria
       'Tito will make Reny cook rice for Ria.'
    d. Mag-pa-pa-lúto'    si  Títo **sa**  katúlong ng    kánin para kay
       AV-CAUS-NB-cook SM Tito DAT helper    ng-P rice   for
       María.
       Maria
       'Tito will make the/a helper cook rice for Maria.'

It is important to note that in (23), Nominative, Dative and ng-P all appear in a sentence.

# Chapter 21

# The particle *sa*: the syntax/semantics continuum

## 21.1. Introduction

The particles *sa* (with common nouns) and *kay* (with human proper nouns) have various functions, including as dative case marker, as preposition of location/direction/source, etc. Blake (1994: 153) introduces the term *local cases* to cover these functions, and remarks that: "the term *local* in this context refers to 'place'. Local cases express notions of location ('at'), destination ('to'), source ('from') and path ('through')." Note that *kay* stands before a singular personal name, while *kina* is used as its plural counterpart.

In the following sections, we shall exemplify sentences in which the particle *sa* is used, where we distinguish the dative *sa* and the prepositional *sa*.

## 21.2. Dative

The particle *sa* has a dative function when it precedes an NP with Recipient and Causee roles. See the following examples.

## 21.2.1. Recipient

(1) a. Nag-bigáy     akó         ng    singsíng  kay  Jóyce.
       AV.FN-give  1SG.NOM  ng-P  ring         DAT  Joyce
       'I gave a ring to Joyce.'

   b. B-in-igy-án         ko            ng    singsíng  si   Jóyce.
                                                               (b-in-igy-án < b-in-igay-án)
       Ci-FN-give-DV  1SG.ng-A  ng-P  ring        SM  Joyce
       'I gave Joyce a ring.'

(2) a. Tu-túlong      akó         sa     áking       iná.
       AV.NB-help  1SG.NOM  DAT  1SG.LK  mother
       'I am going to help my mother.'

   b. Tu-tulúng-an  ko            ang  áking       iná.
       NB-help-DV  1SG.ng-A  SM    1SG.LK  mother
       'I am going to help my mother.'

## 21.2.2. Causee

(3) Mag-pa-pa-patáy         si   Títo  ng    manók      kay  Rény.
    AV-CAUS-NB-kill       SM  Tito  ng-P  chicken  DAT  Reny
    'Tito will make Reny kill a chicken.'

(4) P-in-a-lúto'                    niyá          sa     anák               ang  gúlay.
    Ci-PV.FN-CAUS-cook  3SG.ng-A  DAT  son/daughter  SM    vegetable
    'She made her daughter cook vegetables.'

## 21.3. Other functions

### 21.3.1. Locative

The *sa* phrases in the following examples refer to the place where someone lives or something exists.

(5) a. Saán   ka         naka-tirá?
       where  2SG.NOM   STAT-live
       'Where do you live?'
   b. Naka-tirá  akó        sa  Quezon City.
       STAT-live  1SG.NOM   in  Quezon City
       'I live in Quezon City.'

(6) May    libró  sa  mésa.
    exist  book  on  table
    'There is a book on the table.'

(7) I-p-in-anganák          akó         sa  Fukuoka City. (*anák* 'son/daughter')
    ?-Ci-FN-give.birth  1SG.NOM   in  Fukuoka City
    'I was born in Fukuoka City.'

(8) Mayroóng  laró'  ng    báskétból  mámayá-ng gabí         sa  plása.
                                                                   (English 1986: 783)
    exist.LK  game  GEN  basketball  later-LK  night/evening  in  plaza
    'There is a basketball game this evening in the plaza.'

### 21.3.2.   Directional

The *sa* phrases in the following examples denote the goal to which someone moves. Thus, this use of *sa* is similar to the preposition *to* in English.

(9) P-um-untá       akó         sa  Maynílá'  para  b-um-ilí          ng
    Ci-AV.FN-go  1SG.NOM   to  Manila    for   Ci-AV.NT-buy  ng-P

mga CD.
PL  CD
'I went to Manila to buy CDs.'

(10) Puwéde ka-ng         b-um-isíta    sa ákin kung mínsan.
     allow  2SG.NOM-LK Ci-AV.NT-visit to 1SG if   once
     'You can visit me from time to time.'

### 21.3.3. Time

(11) Ba-balík      akó       sa áking        báyan sa isá-ng   taón.
     AV.NB-return 1SG.NOM to 1SG.GEN.LK home in one-LK year
     'I am going to return to my hometown next year.'

(12) Da-ratíng      siyá       sa Martés.           (English 1986: 1113)
     AV.NB-arrive 3SG.NOM on Tuesday
     'He will arrive on Tuesday.'

### 21.3.4. Cause

(13) Na-ngi-ngínig       sa    gináw        ang báta'.   (English 1986: 1113)
     AV-UF-tremble by/with cold(ness) SM child
     'The child is shaking with cold.'

### 21.3.5. Comitative

(14) S-um-áma           ka        sa    ákin.            (English 1986: 1113)
     Ci-AV.IMP-follow 2SG.NOM with/to 1SG
     'Come with me.'

## 21.4. Tagalog *sa* and Japanese *ni* compared

As shown in the preceding sections, the particle **sa** in Tagalog has various functions. It expresses the dative meaning, as well as direction, location, goal/source, etc. This is also true of the particle *ni* in Japanese, which expresses dative, direction, location, source, etc. It is interesting to note that the *ni* particle marks the passive agent. I will classify the passive agent marked with *ni* into dative, although it resembles source in function. Note, in relation to this, that the particle *kara* 'from' can be sometimes used instead of the passive agent *ni*, as seen in (17) below. The following examples from Japanese pinpoint the parallelism between the particles *sa* and *ni* in these two languages.

### 21.4.1. Dative

(15) Taroo ga    Hanako ni    yubiwa o    age-ta.
     Taro NOM  Hanako DAT  ring    ACC  give-PAST
     'Taro gave a ring to Hanako.'

(16) Nori ga    Maria ni    tegami o    kai-ta.
     Nori NOM  Maria DAT  letter   ACC  write-PAST
     'Nori wrote a letter to Maria.'

(17) Nori ga    Miruku    ni/kara    kam-are-ta.
     Nori NOM  Milk (cat)  DAT/from  bite-PASS-PAST
     'Nori was bitten by Milk.'

### 21.4.2. Locative

(18) Watasi wa    itumo    UP no    yunibaasitii hoteru ni
     1SG    TM   always   UP GEN  University   Hotel  LOC

tomari-masu.
stay-POL(UF)
'I stay at the University Hotel on the UP campus (whenever I visit the Philippines).'

(19) Heya ni    takusan (no)   hon   ga    ari-masu.
    room LOC many   (GEN) book NOM exist-POL(UF)
    'There are many books in the room.'

### 21.4.3. Time
(20) Tuki   ni    itido  wa   ryokoo-si-tai.
    month TIME once TM travel-do-DES
    'I want to travel once a month.'

### 21.4.4. Directional
(21) Nori wa   rainen    amerika ni   ryuugaku-suru    yotei desu.
    Nori TM next.year America DIR studing.abroad-do plan COP
    'Nori is going to study in America next year.'
(22) Yumi wa   ookiku   nat-tara   isya   ni     naru   tumori
    Yumi TM grown.up become-if doctor DIR/goal become intention
    desu.
    COP
    'Yumi intends to be a doctor when she has grown up.'

# Part IV

# Miscellaneous

# Chapter 22

# Ability/Permission

## 22.1. Introduction

The notion of 'ability' in English is conveyed by the auxiliary verb *can*. Permission may be expressed by the auxiliary verb *may* or *can*. Colloquial Tagalog expresses the notion of 'ability' by the forms *mahúsay* 'good', *magalíng* 'excellent, good' and *marúnong* 'able, talented', and the notion of 'permission' by the form *puwéde* 'may' or *maaári* 'may'. The notion of ability in Tagalog can also be expressed by the verbal prefix *maka-*, which inflects for aspects.

In this chapter, we deal with the expressions of ability, permission and prohibition. In English, the notion of 'prohibition' is expressed by the form *don't*, while in Tagalog it is expressed by the form *huwág* or *bawál*. Note that both in Tagalog and English, infinitive or neutral forms of a verb follow these forms. English (1986: 671) states, however, that the sequence of *huwág* and an inceptive form of a verb often makes the prohibition milder so that it is almost equivalent to a request: *Huwág kayóng magágálit* 'Don't get angry'. In the following sections, I will explain expressions of these notions by giving illustrative sentences in the order of ability, permission and prohibition. Incidentally, *puwéde* and *huwág* are often spelled *pwéde* and *hwág*, respectively. But we use *puwéde* and *huwág*, given in Ramos (1971b). Incidentally, the notions of 'ability' and 'permission' lack the imperative form for semantic reasons. Note that they denote events and happen spontaneously. The notion of 'prohibition' is regarded as a negative command.

## 22.2. Ability

The notion of ability in Tagalog can be expressed in several ways, as shown below.

( 1 ) She can swim very well.
    a. Magalíng siyá-ng l-um-angóy.
       excellent 3SG.NOM-LK Ci-AV.NT-swim.
    b. Naká-ka-langóy siyá-ng nang mahúsay/mabúti.
       AV.able-UF-swim 3SG.NOM-LK ADVL good
    c. Naka-lá-langóy siyá nang mahúsay/mabúti.
       AV.able-UF-swim 3SG.NOM ADVL good

The form *nang*, pronounced [naŋ], is used to form an adverb from an adjective, when it must precede the adjective. Thus, we call the form *nang* adverbializer (ADVL). Ms Manueli, one of my Tagalog consultants, comments that the (1c) form above is used more generally than the (1b) form. For the sake of reference, I have marked the stress in the reduplicated (C)V in (1c), although it is predictable. Now observe the following.

( 2 ) She can cook very well.
    a. Magalíng siyá-ng mag-lúto'.
       excellent 3SG.NOM-LK AV.NT-cook
    b. Naka-ka-lúto' siyá nang mahúsay/mabúti.
    c. Naka-lu-lúto' siyá nang mahúsay/mabúti.
    d. Naka-ka-*pag*-lúto' siyá nang mabúti.

e. Naka-*pag*-lu-lúto' siyá nang mabúti.

( 3 ) They can speak Tagalog very well.
    a. Marúnong silá-ng          mag-salitá'    ng    Tagálog.
        talented     3PL.NOM-LK AV.NT-speak ng-P Tagalog
    b. Magalíng silá-ng          mag-salitá'    ng    Tagálog.
        excellent    3PL.NOM-LK AV.NT-speak ng-P Tagalog
    c. Naka-ka-*pag*-salitá' silá ng Tagálog nang mabúti.
    d. Naka-*pag*-sa-salitá' silá ng Tagálog nang mabúti.
    (Note that 'to speak Tagalog' can also be expressed by the form *managálog*.)

Note that *marunong* 'able, talented' and *magaling* 'talented' consist of the adjectival prefix *ma-* and the root words *dunong* and *galing*, respectively, as discussed in Chapter 16. We see from (2d-e) and (3c-d) that in the expression of ability, *-pag-* can be inserted between *maka-* and a verb form which usually derives a *mag-* verb from a root word. This is also shown in the following examples.

( 4 ) Her daughter can read a book, although she is only five years old.
    a. Marúnong nang       mag-bása     ang anák niyá-ng
        able          already-LK AV.NT-read SM child 3SG.GEN-LK
        babáe    káhit na limá-ng taón pa    lang siyá.
        woman   though   five-LK year still only 3SG.NOM
    b. Naka-ka-bása ng libró ang anák niyá-ng babáe káhit na limá-ng taón pa lang siyá.
    c. Naka-ba-bása ng libró ang anák niyá-ng babáe káhit na limá-ng taón pa lang siyá.
    d. Naka-ka-*pag*-bása ng libró ang anák niyá-ng babáe káhit na limá-ng taón pa lang siyá.

e. Naka-*pag*-ba-bása ng libró ang anák niyá-ng babáe káhit na limá-ng taón pa lang siyá.

(5) Can you hit me on the head?
Ma-ta-tamá'-an     mo          ba akó         sa úlo?
able-NB-hit-DIR  2SG.ng-A   Q  1SG.NOM    on head

(6) Tony will not be able to pay, because he has no money.
Hindí maka-ka-(*pag*-)báyad si    Tóny dáhil    walá'
not    AV.able-NB-pay         SM  Tony  because nothing
siyá-ng            péra.
3SG.NOM-LK   money

Recall that various forms are used to express the notion of 'ability' if they are compatible with the context.

## 22.3. Permission

(7) You can enter the classroom even on Sunday.
Puwéde ka-ng                 p-um-ások       sa (loób ng)   silíd-aralán
possible 2SG.NOM-LK   Ci-AV.NT-enter  in (inside of)  classroom
káhit   Linggó.
even   Sunday

(8) Can I sleep earlier?
Puwéde/Maaári' ba   akó-ng              ma-túlog         nang     maága?
possible              Q  1SG.NOM-LK    AV.NT-sleep  ADVL    early

(9) Can I eat earlier than you?

a. Puwéde ba na    ma-uná         akó-ng         k-um-áin
   possible Q already AV.NT-precede 1SG.NOM-LK Ci-AV.NT-eat
   sa iyó?
   to 2SG
b. Ma-u-uná     na    akó-ng         k-um-áin      sa iyó.
   AV-NB-precede already 1SG.NOM-LK Ci-AV.NT-eat to 2SG

(10) Yes, you can visit Japan.
   Oo,  puwéde ka-ng        b-um-isíta       sa Hapón.
   yes  can    2SG.NOM-LK Ci-AV.NT-visit to Japan

(11) Can I go home, cutting my class?
   a. Puwéde na    ba akó-ng       um-uwí'?
      possible already Q 1SG.NOM-LK AV.NT-go.home
      'Can I go home?'
      Hindí' na     akó       pa-pások    sa su-sunód    na kláse.
      not   already 1SG.NOM AV.NB-enter in AV.NB-follow LK class
      'I won't attend the next class.' (NB: *su-sunód* 'following')
   b. Puwéde ba akó-ng       um-uwí'        nang    maága,
      possible Q 1SG.NOM-LK AV.NT-go home   ADVL    early
      i-ka-kat      ko         ang  kláse ko.
      PV-NB-cut 1SG.ng-A SM class 1SG.GEN

## 22.4. Prohibition

Prohibition can be seen as a negative command. In Tagalog, it is expressed by the form *huwág* or *bawál* followed by the neutral form. As indicated in Section 22.1, *huwág* can also be followed by the inceptive form to soften prohibition (English 1986: 671). (Ms Salazar does not agree with this idea.) The following are examples of *huwág*.

(12) Don't go shopping downtown.
Huwág ka-ng ma-milí sa dáwntawn.
(ma-milí < maN-bilí 'to buy')
don't 2SG.NOM-LK AV.NT-shop to downtown

(13) Don't give money to the children, because money spoils them.
Huwág (ka-ng) ma-migáy ng péra sa mga
don't (2SG.NOM-LK) AV.NT-dispense ng-P money DAT PL
báta', dáhil naka-ka-síra' sa kanilá ang péra.
(mamigáy < maN-bigáy 'to give')
child because AV-UF-spoil/break DAT 3PL SM money

(14) Don't give food to the fish.
Huwág/Báwal mag-bigáy/mag-tápon ng pagkáin sa
don't/prohibitive AV.NT-give/AV.NT-throw.away ng-P food DAT
isdá'.
fish
(This was from a notice found in the Japanese Garden in Manila in 1974.)

## 22.5. Conjugation of *maka-* verbs

The conjugation patterns of *maka-* verbs are listed in Aspillera (1969: 57), from which the following table was adapted.

Table 22–1: Conjugation of *maka-* verbs

| Root Word | túlog 'to sleep' | lígo' 'to bathe' |
|---|---|---|
| Neutral | maka-túlog | maka-lígo' |
| Imperative | none | none |
| Perfective | naka-túlog | naka-lígo' |
| Imperfective | naka-tu-túlog/ naka-ka-túlog | naka-li-lígo'/ naka-ka-lígo' |
| Inceptive | maka-tu-túlog/ maka-ka-túlog | maka-li-lígo'/ maka-ka-lígo' |

## 22.6. Stative: *naka-*

In this section, we deal with the prefix *naka-*, because it formally resembles the prefix *maka-*, although it does not have to do with the notions dealt with so far. The prefix *naka-* differs from the perfective form of ability *maka-*. In contrast to ability *maka-*, *naka-* does not conjugate and denotes a state of action expressed by a root word. The root word marked with the prefix *naka-* is in the agent-voice, as shown in the following examples adapted from Aspillera (1969: 112).

(15) Naka-tayó' sa tabí ng pintó' ang áking iná. (BT: 112)
    AV.STAT-stand by side GEN door SM 1SG.GEN.LK mother
    'My mother is standing by the door.'

(16) Kailángang naka-sapátos ang báta' sa pag-la-láro'. (BT: 112)
    necessary.LK AV.STAT-shoes SM child in NML-play
    'The children need to wear shoes while playing.'

Note that as in (16), *naka-* can be prefixed on root words like 'shirts', 'glasses', etc. The verbs denote what one wears: e.g. *naka-salamín* 'wear or have glasses'. Even *naka-kótse* 'travel by car' is possible.

# Chapter 23

# Auxiliary-like verbs

## 23.1. Introduction

In Chapter 4, we took a brief look at the *Gusto*-construction. In this chapter, we deal with auxiliary-like verb constructions in general.

First of all, it must be made clear why we use the term auxiliary-like verb instead of the term auxiliary verb. The reason is that Tagalog does not have genuine auxiliary verbs. Admittedly, auxiliary-like verbs are followed by the neutral forms of verbs as in English. But they can also be used as genuine verbs, as indicated by (1b) and (1c) below. In addition, certain auxiliary-like verbs conjugate (cf. (3c) and (6c)) and change voice and aspect (cf. (1d)). What is more, the agent NPs (more specifically, experiencer NPs) that follow *gusto* 'like' and *ibig* 'like' must be in the ng-A case even when the embedded clauses are agent-voiced, as seen in (1a) (see Aspillera 1969: 52).

## 23.2. Examples

### 23.2.1. *gustó*: like

The following are examples of the *gusto*-constructions. The *gusto* forms in (1b) and (1c) serve as genuine verbs. Note the difference between (1b) and (1c) in meaning. Thus, I glossed the *ang* particle in (1c) as DET/NOM.

(1) a. Gustó  kong            k-um-áin       ng    tinápay.
       like   1SG.ng-A.LK     Ci-AV.NT-eat   ng-P  bread
       'I want to eat some bread.'
    b. Gustó  ng      babáe    ng     ságing.
       like   ng-A    woman    ng-P   banana
       'The girl wants bananas.'
    c. Gustó  ng      babáe    ang       ságing.
       like   ng-A    woman    DET/NOM   banana
       'The girl wants the banana.'
    d. G-in-ustó        niya-ng         um-akyát    sa   bundók.
       Ci-PV.FN-like    3SG.ng-A.LK     AV.NT-climb to   mountain.
       'S/he wanted to climb the mountain.'

*Gusto* must be followed by ng-A forms, without reference to the voice in embedded clauses. It is not clear what makes a difference between *gusto* in (1a) and *ginusto* in (1d).

As discussed in Chapter 20, *ng-A* and *ng-P* are different in function. See the following examples.

(2) a. Gustó-ng  k-um-áin       ng     báta'.           (English 1986: 167)
       like-LK   Ci-AV.NT-eat   ng-A   child.
       'The child wants to eat.'
    b. Gustó-ng  um-inóm       ng     gátas  ng     báta'.         (BT: 53)
       like-LK   AV.NT-drink   ng-P   milk   ng-A   child
       'The child wants to drink milk.'

It is to be noted that in (2b) *ng* forms appear sequentially, where *ng gatas* functions as P and *ng bata'* functions as A.

### 23.2.2.  *kailángan* : need

The form *kelángan* is sometimes used colloquially or in rapid speech. For more information on this, see Chapter 2 'Phonology'.

( 3 ) a. Kailángan  náting            mag-áral         nang    mabúti.
        need       2PL.INCL.ng-A.LK  AV.NT-study     ADVL    good
        'We (INCL) need to study hard.'
    b.  Kailángan  ko-ng          p-um-ások        sa   opisína   búkas.
        need       1SG.ng-A-LK    Ci-AV.NT-enter   to   office    tomorrow
        'I need to go to the office tomorrow.'
    c.  Ka-kailangán-in  ng     mga   báta'   na   ma-lígo'        sa   ílog.
        NB-need-PV       ng-A   PL    child   LK   AV.NT-bathe    in   river
        'The children will need to take a bath in the river.'

Note that in the examples above, *kailangan* is followed by the *ng-A* form, despite the fact that the following clause is agent-voiced.

### 23.2.3.  *dápat* : must, should

( 4 ) a.  Dápat  silá-ng         mag-maného   nang     maáyos.
         must   3PL.NOM-LK      AV.NT-drive  ADVL    orderly
         'They must drive carefully.'

b. Dápat  táyo-ng              mag-lakád    nang    mabilís.
   must    1PL.INCL.NOM-LK    AV.NT-walk   ADVL    fast
   'We (INCL) must walk fast.'

### 23.2.4.  *maaári'*: **may, allowed**

(5) a. Maaári' ba akó-ng            t-um-akbó?
       may     Q  1SG.NOM-LK       Ci-AV.NT-run
       'May I run?'

   b. Maaári-ng kaín-in      ang tinápay sa mésa.
      may-LK    eat-PV.NT    SM  bread   on table
      '(You) may eat the bread on the table.'

A word must be said about (5b), because one of my consultants translated (5b) as 'The bread on the table may be eaten'. This means that the form *sa mesa* is ambiguous between the place of eating and the place of bread. More accurately, *the bread that is on the table* is *ang tinapay na nasa mesa* in Tagalog.

### 23.2.5.  *puwéde*: **may, permitted**

The phonological structure of *puwéde* tells us that it is a borrowed word. Nevertheless, this form is used more frequently than *maaári'*. The latter form is native and sounds quite formal.

(6) a. Puwéde ba akó-ng        s-um-áma       sa   iyó   sa
       may    Q  1SG.NOM-LK   Ci-AV.NT-join  with 2SG   to
       Japán/Hapón?
       Japan
       'Can I go with you to Japan?'

   b. Puwéde ka-ng          mag-laró'   sa  labás.
      may    2SG.NOM-LK    AV.NT-play  in  outside

'You can play outside.'
c. Pu-puwéde ka-ng       um-alís      nang   maága.
   NB-may    2SG.NOM-LK AV.NT-leave ADVL   fast
   'You will be allowed to go early./You can go early.'

## 23.2.6. *hindí' puwéde*: **not allowed**

Finally, we show the negative use of auxiliary-like verbs, taking *hindí' puwéde* as an example.

(7) Hindí' puwéde-ng    i-pása     ang gawá' mo.
    not   allowed-LK PV.NT-pass SM  work  2SG.GEN/ng-A
    'Your work cannot be licensed.'

# Chapter 24

# Adverbs

## 24.1. Introduction

Adverbs can be formed by placing *nang* before adjectives. We call the form *nang* adverbializer (ADVL). *Nang* is pronounced [naŋ], which suggests an affinity to the case marker *ng*. When an adjective occurs sentence-initially and is followed by a clause, the adjective functions as a sentential modifier, where the linker *-ng* or *na* appears to connect the adjective and the modified clause. Thus, Tagalog has two types of adverbial expression, as seen in (1).

( 1 ) a. Mabilís (na) t-um-akbó si Ichíro.
    fast (LK) Ci-AV.NT-run SM Ichiro
    'Ichiro runs fast.'
  b. T-um-a-takbó si Ichíro nang mabilís.
    Ci-AV-UF-run SM Ichiro ADVL fast
    'Ichiro runs fast.' or 'Ichiro is running fast.'

Note that the linker *na* is often dropped, as in (1a), while the linker *-ng* is not dropped (Ramos and Cena 1990: 71). The alternation between *na* and *-ng* depends on the preceding sound. We call the first type *sentential adverbs* (1a) and the second type *nang-adverbs* (1b). When a (personal) pronoun is used as the subject in the type of *sentential adverb*, it comes after a sentential adverb, as illustrated below.

( 2 )  Mabilís siyá-ng t-um-akbó.
      fast 3SG.NOM-LK Ci-AV.NT-run
      'S/he runs fast.'

As is clear in (1a) and (1b), the sentence with a sentential adverb can be formalized as *Adjective + Linker + Modified Clause*, whereas the sentence with a *nang*-adverb as *Clause + nang Adjective*.

It is worth mentioning that sentential adverbs and *nang*-adverbs do not necessarily alternate with each other. In Section 24.2, we shall show examples in which sentential adverbs and *nang*-adverbs are interchangeable, and in Section 24.3, we shall show examples in which they are not. In Section 24.4, we shall examine what determines the interchangeability.

## 24.2. Examples of sentential-adverbs/nang-adverbs

The following are examples in which both sentential adverbs and *nang*-adverbs are accepted.

( 3 )  a. Masípag siyá-ng mag-áral ng mga wíka'.
        diligent 3SG.NOM-LK AV.NT-study ng-P PL language
        'S/he studies languages diligently.'
     b. Nag-a-áral siyá ng mga wíka' nang masípag.
        AV-UF-study 3SG.NOM ng-P PL language ADVL diligent
        'S/he studies languages diligently.'

(4) a. Mabilís (na) mag-tayp si Ann.
       fast    (LK) AV.NT-type SM Ann
       'Ann types fast.'
    b. Nag-ta-tayp si Ann nang mabilís.
       AV-UF-type SM Ann ADVL fast
       'Ann types fast.' or 'Ann is typing fast.'

## 24.3. Examples of sentential adverbs/*nang-adverb

The following are examples that do not accept *nang*-adverbs but accept sentential adverbs.

(5) 'Reymond always visits us at home.'
    a. Palági-ng p-um-u-puntá sa áming báhay si Reymond.
       always-LK $C_i$-AV-UF-go to 1PL.EXCL.GEN.LK house SM Reymond
    b. P-um-u-puntá sa áming báhay si Reymond palági'.
       $C_i$-AV-UF-go to 1PL.EXCL.GEN.LK house SM Reymond always
    c.*P-um-u-puntá sa áming báhay si Reymond nang palági'.
       $C_i$-AV-UF-go to 1PL.EXCL.GEN.LK house SM Reymond ADVL always

(6) 'David certainly arrives tomorrow.' or 'It is certain that David arrives tomorrow.'
    a. Tiyák na da-ratíng si David búkas.
       certain LK AV.NB-arrive SM David tomorrow

b. ⁽*⁾Da-ratíng si David búkas nang tiyák.
   AV.NB-arrive SM David tomorrow ADVL certain

(7) a. Sobrá-ng ma-túlog ang púsa'.
   much-LK AV.NT-sleep SM cat
   'The cat sleeps so much.'

b. ⁽*⁾Na-tu-túlog ang púsa' nang sobrá.
   AV-UF-sleep SM cat ADVL much

## 24.4. Interchangeability

To make it clear what determines the interchangeability between sentential adverbs and *nang*-adverbs, it is necessary to compare the examples in Section 24.2 with those in Section 24.3, with a focus on their semantic difference.

(8) *masípag* 'diligent', *mabilís* 'fast'
   a. ADJ + LK + CL (neutral V)
   b. V + NP + ... *nang* ADJ

(9) *palági* 'always'
   a. ADJ + LK + CL (neutral V/conjugated V)
   b. *V + NP + ... *nang* ADJ

It is clear from schemata (8) and (9) above that Tagalog, in fact, has two types of adverbial construction. Note that *palagi*, etc., cannot be preceded by the adverbializer *nang*. This type can be regarded as genuine adverbs. Another type originally functions as adjective. See *masipag*, *mabilis*, etc., where the adjectival prefix *ma-* is involved.

Now we focus our attention on their semantic difference.

(10) a. Either construction: masípag 'diligent', mabilís 'fast', etc.
    b. Sentential only: palági 'always, often', etc.

It turns out that the difference is closely related to the meaning. Adverbs like *masípag* 'diligent' and *mabilís* 'fast' express a property of the agent, which can be considered as adverbs of manner. In contrast, we cannot say *\*nang palagi* 'always', which express frequency. More data will be needed to conclude the point at issue (for verbal modification, see Ramos and Cena 1990: 71).

## 24.5. Structures of sentential adverbs and related constructions

We are now in a better position to examine the structures of sentential adverb constructions and auxiliary-like verb constructions with *gustó* 'like' and *puwéde* 'may', because they are similar in structure. See the following schema, which explicitly shows their affinity.

(11) a. Gusto  
    b. Masipag  } + Linker + Embedded Clause (V: Neutral)

Schema (11) indicates that they have an embedded clause preceded by the linker whose verb form is neutral in aspect.

# Chapter 25

# Existentials and possessives: *may*

## 25.1. Introduction

It is a well-known fact that there are two types of language in expressing existentials and possessives. One type includes languages that use a verb common to both constructions and the other type includes languages that do not. English belongs to the latter type, because existentials are expressed by the *there*-construction, while possessives are by the *have*-construction, as shown in (1).

(1) a. *There* are a lot of books on the table.   (Existential)
    b. The students *have* a lot of books.   (Possessive)

The typical example of the former type is Chinese, where *yǒu* is used to express existentials and possessives (Li and Thompson 1981).

It is interesting to note that existentials and possessives are semantically related to each other. Existentials explicitly denote a place where something or someone exists, while possessives entail a person, instead of a place, who possesses something or someone. Thus, the difference between them lies in who has something or where something exists. The formal difference between them comes from this semantic difference. Tagalog belongs to the Chinese type, because the form *may* is used to express existentials and possessives.

## 25.2. The *may* form

Tagalog uses the form *may* to express both existentials and possessives. This reflects a semantic parallelism between these two constructions. Thus, we shall call existentials and possessives in Tagalog just ***may* construction**. Examples (2) through (4) below illustrate the *may* constructions, where the (a) sentences are existentials and the (b) sentences are possessives. Needless to say, the *may* constructions semantically presuppose that there exists something or someone (who possesses something/someone). Note that existentials have no *ang*-marked NPs.

( 2 ) a. May marámi-ng libró sa mésa.
       exist many-LK book on table
       'There are a lot of books on the table.'
   b. May marámi-ng libró ang mga estudyánte.
       exist many-LK book SM PL student
       'The students have a lot of books.'

( 3 ) a. May marámi-ng péra sa bángko.
       exist much-LK money in bank
       'There is much money in the bank.'
   b. May marámi-ng pera siyá.
       exist much-LK money 3SG.NOM
       'S/he has a lot of money.'

( 4 ) a. May limá-ng *báta'* sa báhay niyá.
       exist five-LK child in house 3SG.GEN

'There are five children in his/her house.'

b. May limá-ng *anák* silá.
   exist five-LK son/daughter 3PL.NOM
   'They have five children.'

Incidentally, Tagalog has two different words for 'child', since semantically *child* has two different meanings, 'offspring' and 'young person'. In Tagalog, *anák* is used for 'offspring', and *báta'* for 'a young person'. The use of these two words can be made clear by the examples in (5) below.

(5) a. Iláng *báta'* sa párke?
   how many.LK child in park
   'How many *children* are *there* in the park?'

b. Iláng *anák* mo?  < Ilán ang anák mo?
   how many.LK child 2SG.GEN
   'How many *children* do you *have*?'

## 25.3. The *mayroón* form

The form *mayroón* consists of two words: *may* 'exist' and *doón* 'there'. Aspillera (1969: 36) suggests that *may* is replaced by the form *mayroón* pronounced [mayro'ón] or [mero(')ón] when

(6) a. it is followed by a monosyllabic particle such as *na*, *pa*, *ba*, etc., as in (7a).
   b. it is followed by personal pronouns, as in (7b).
   c. answering *may/mayroón* questions affirmatively, as seen in (7c) below.

The following are examples of the *mayroón* constructions.

(7) a. Mayroón **ba** silá-ng      bágo-ng aklát?            (BT: 36)
       exist      Q  3PL.NOM-LK new-LK book
       'Do they have a new book?'
   b. Mayroón **kayó**-ng      bágo-ng kótse?
      exist      2PL.NOM-LK new-LK car
      'Do you have a new car?'
   c. May asáwa ba si Tóny?  **Oo**, mayroón.
      exist spouse Q SM Tony  yes exist
      'Does Tony have a wife?' 'Yes, he does.'

## 25.4. The *walá* form

When answering *may/mayroon* questions negatively, the form *walá* 'none' is used. Note that the form *hindí* 'no/not' cannot be used as a negative answer to *may/mayroon* questions. (8b) is an example of a negative answer.

(8) a. Mayroón ka         ba-ng diksiyunáryo-ng Japanese-Taglog?
       exist     2SG.NOM Q-LK dictionary-LK     Japanese-Tagalog
       'Do you have a Japanese-Tagalog Dictionary?'
    b. Walá'. Walá' akó-ng       diksiyunáryo-ng Japanese-Tagalog.
       none  none 1SG.NOM-LK dictionary-LK     Japanese-Tagalog.
       'No, I don't have a Japanese-Tagalog dictionary.'

# Chapter 26

# Subjectless sentences

## 26.1. Introduction

English has a dummy subject *it*, which is used to express meteorology, darkness/brightness, difficulty/ease, etc. The same is true of German, which has an empty subject *es* 'it'. The German equivalent of 'it rains' is *es regnet* 'it rains'. Thus, we tend to assume that the dummy subject phenomenon is common to European languages, which are often called subject prominent languages (Li and Thompson 1976). Note, however, that Sanskrit, Greek, Latin, Russian, etc., do not use a dummy subject to express meteorology.

It is important to note that Tagalog does not use any empty subject. In this chapter, we examine subjectless sentences in the language. To put it another way, we do not examine sentences with *ang*-marked NPs, with the exception of *ang*-marked exclamations.

Incidentally, these expressions may be relatable to the transitivity hierarchy of verbs. That is, verbs used in subjectless sentences are low in this hierarchy.

## 26.2. Subjectless sentences: examples

The empty subject *it* in English is used in the constructions that express meteorology, temperature, etc. In Tagalog, these expressions are formed by subjectless sentences. By the same token, extraposition is not possible in Tagalog, since the language has no dummy subject.

Illustrative sentences will serve to explain what the subjectless sentences look like.

### 26.2.1. Meteorology

( 1 ) a. Um-ulán    kahápon. (RW *ulán*: noun 'rain')
     AV.FN-rain yesterday
     'It rained yesterday.'

   b. Um-u-ulán   sa Marikína.
     AV-UF-rain in Marikina
     'It is raining in Marikina.'

( 2 ) a. Um-áraw    sa ámin. (RW: *araw* noun 'sun, day')
     AV.FN-shine in 1PL.EXCL
     'The sun shone in our place.'

   b. Um-a-áraw   sa búkid palági'.
     AV-UF-shine in field always
     'It is always sunny in the field.'

( 3 ) a. Maínit díto sa Maynílaʼ.
     hot    here in Manila
     'It is hot here in Manila.'

   b. Maínit **ang** Mayníla.
     hot     SM Manila

'It is hot in Manila.'
   c. Maínit  sa kuwárto.
      hot     in room
      'It is hot in the room'
   d. Um-i-ínit  sa palígid.
      AV-UF-hot in vicinity
      'It is getting hot around here.'
   e. Um-ínit    kanína.
      AV.FN-hot just before
      'It was hot a moment ago.'

(4) a. Malamíg dito.
     cold    here
     'It is cold here.'
   b. Malamíg **ang** panahón.
     cold     SM  weather/time
     'The weather is cold.'

Note that example (3b) above has an *ang*-marked NP as an alternative to *sa*, although the *ang*-marked NP denotes the place where the phenomenon at issue can be found. This use of *ang* needs further study.

### 26.2.2. Darkness/brightness

(5) a. Maliwánag sa kuwárto námin.
     bright    in room   1PL.EXCL.GEN
     'It is bright in our room.'
   b. Maliwánag **ang** ílaw.
     bright     SM  light
     'The light is bright.'

(6) a. Madilím sa kámpus.
      dark    on campus
      'It is dark on campus.'
  b. Madilím na.
      dark    already
      'It is already dark.'

### 26.2.3. Natural phenomena

(7) a. L-um-i-lindól palági' sa California.
      $C_i$-AV-UF-earthquake always in California
      'There's always an earthquake in California.'
  b. L-um-indól kahápon.
      AV-FN-earthquake yesterday
      'There was an earthquake yesterday.'

(8) a. B-um-agyó sa Baguio.
      AV-FN-storm in Baguio
      'There was a storm in Baguio.'
  b. L-um-ampás na **ang** bagyó.    (English 1986: 117)
      Ci-AV.FN-pass already SM typhoon
      'The typhoon has passed.'

## 26.3. Recently finished

The notion that an action has just finished or recently finished is termed 'recently-finished' (RF). This notion is expressed in Tagalog by a subjectless sentence in which the prefix *ka-* is prefixed on the verb stem with reduplication of the initial (C)V of the RW, which can be represented by the following schema:

(9) Recently-Finished: *ka + RED + RW + ng-A + (V: NT) + (ng-P)*

The following are examples of 'recently-finished'.

(10) a. Ka-ta-tápos          ko            lang mag-lúto'      ng      isdá'.
         RF-RED-finish   1SG.ng-A just   AV.NT-cook   ng-P fish
         'I have just finished cooking fish.'
    b. Ka-li-línis       lang námin              ng     báhay.
         RF-RED-clean just  1PL.EXCL.ng-A ng-P house
         'We have just finished cleaning a house.'
    c. Ka-ra-ratíng      lang ni            Tóny gáling sa kláse.
                                                                    (ratíng < datíng)
         RF-RED-arrive just  PN.SG.ng-A Tony from       class
         'Tony has just arrived from class.'

## 26.4. Exclamation

Exclamatory sentences in Tagalog take the form *ano-LK + RW + GEN/ng-A* or the form *kay + RW + GEN/ng-A*. Both *ang* and *kay* in this construction can be glossed as EXC (exclamation).

(11) a. Anó-ng     gandá ni                  Tína!
         EXC-LK  beauty PN.SG.GEN/ng-A Tina
         'What a beautiful lady Tina is!'
    b. Kay    gandá ni                  Tína!
         EXC  beauty PN.SG.GEN/ng-A Tina
         'How beautiful Tina is!'

(12) a. Anó-ng    taás         ng              Mayón!
       EXC-LK   highness   GEN/ng-A   Mayon volcano
       'What a high mountain Mt. Mayon is!'
   b. Kay    taás         ng              Mayón!
       EXC   highness   GEN/ng-A   Mayon
       'How high Mt. Mayon is!'

Additionally, Ramos and Cena (1990: 39) illustrate the following examples.

(13) a. Ang    bilís     ng              babáe!
       EXC    speed   GEN/ng-A   woman
       'How fast the woman is!'
   b. Ang    bilís    t-um-akbó              ni                    Ben!
       EXC    speed   Ci-AV.NT/FN-run   PN.SG.GEN/ng-A   Ben
       'How fast Ben ran (runs)!'

These examples except (13b) can be seen as nominalizations, since the GEN or ng-A form follows the root word, where the particles *ang* and *kay* function as a nominalizer.

Note, finally, that constructions such as sentential adverbs, auxiliary-like verbs and existentials are also included under the rubric of subjectless sentences.

# Chapter 27

# Conjunctions

## 27.1. Introduction

Conjunctions are linguistic devices used to connect a word with a word, a phrase with a phrase, a clause with a clause, etc., and are useful for conveying a full range of information. In this chapter, we shall illustrate coordinating and subordinating conjunctions. As will be clear from examples that follow, some subordinating conjunctions can be used as prepositions as well.

## 27.2. Coordinating conjunctions

### 27.2.1. *at* : and

( 1 ) a. Maulán *at* malamíg ang panahón ngayón.
      rainy and cold SM weather today
      'The weather is rainy and cold today.'

  b. Estudyánte ng UP si Tína *at* (sáka) nag-a-áral
     student GEN UP SM Tina and (then) AV-UF-study
     siyá ng linguistíka nang masípag.
     3SG.NOM ng-P linguistics ADVL diligent

'Tina is a student at UP and studies linguistics very hard.'
c. Nag-lúto' ang nánay ng adóbo *at* k-in-áin ng
    AV.FN-cook SM mother ng-P adobo and Ci-PV.FN-eat ng-A
    tátay.
    father
    'Mother cooked adobo and father ate (it).'

It is interesting to note that in the second clause of (1c), *ang adobo* is deleted. Note that *adobo* serves as ng-P in the first clause while it serves as the subject in the second clause. Thus, P in the first clause triggers deletion of the *ang*-marked NP in the second clause. The same is true of example (2a) below. This phenomenon cannot be treated in terms of accusative analysis.

### 27.2.2. *péro, ngúnit*: but

(2) a. B-um-ilí kamí ng guntíng *péro* hindí'
    Ci-AV.FN-buy 1PL.EXCL.NOM ng-P scissors but not
    g-um-a-gána.
    C$_i$-AV-UF-function
    'We bought a pair of scissors but (it) doesn't work.

b. A-alís akó *ngúnit* ba-balík akó
   AV.NB-leave 1SG.NOM but AV.NB-return 1SG.NOM
   agád. (English 1986: 945)
   immediately
   'I'll be leaving but I'll be back straight away.'

### 27.2.3. *o*: or

(3) a. A-alís ka ba *o* mag-pa-paíwan?
    AV.NB-leave 2SG.NOM Q or AV-NB-stay
    'Are you going or (are you) staying?'

b. Matamís ba *o* maásim? (English 1986: 946)
sweet Q or sour
'Is it sweet or sour?'

c. Mansánas *o* úbas ang masaráp kaín-in?
apple or grape SM good eat-NT.PV
'Are apples or grapes nice to eat?'

## 27.3. Subordinating conjunctions

### 27.3.1. *nang, kung, kapag, noon*: when

(4) a. Nag-ba-bása ng diyáryo si Kíko' *nang* um-alís si
AV-UF-read ng-P newspaper SM Kiko when AV.NT-leave SM
Vícky.
Vicky
'Kiko was reading a newspaper when Vicky left.'

b. *Nang* maliít akó, may dalawá-ng púsa' akó.
when small 1SG.NOM exist two-LK cat 1SG.NOM
'When I was young, I had two cats.'

c. *Nang* ma-matáy ang báta' ay um-iyák nang um-iyák
when AV.NT-die SM child TM AV.FN-cry EMP AV.FN-cry
ang iná.
SM mother
'When the child died the mother cried and cried.' (English 1977: 928)

d. *Nang* sabí-hin niyá iyón ay na-gálit akó.
(English 1977: 1183)
when say-NT.PV 3SG.ng-A that TM AV-FN 1SG.NOM
'When he said that, I got angry.'

( 5 ) *Kung* a-alís ka, sa-sáma akó sa iyó.
(BT: 83)
If AV.NB-leave 2SG.NOM AV.NB-join 1SG.NOM with 2SG
'If/when you leave, I will go with you.'

( 6 ) a. *Kapág* t-um-íla' ang ulán, puwéde ka-ng
when Ci-AV.FN-stop SM rain may 2SG.NOM-LK
um-uwí'.
AV.NT-go home
'When it stops raining, you can go home.'
b. *Kapág* na-ga-gálit siyá ay l-um-a-labás
when AV-UF-get.angry 3SG.NOM TM Ci-AV-UF-go.out
akó sa silíd.
1SG.NOM from room
'Whenever he gets angry, I go out of the room.' (English 1986: 298)

( 7 ) *Noong* nag-ta-trabáho siyá sa Maynílaʼ, akóʼy
when.LK AV-UF-work 3SG.NOM in Manila 1SG.NOM-TM
nása probínsya.
in province
'When he was working in Manila, I was in the province.'
(English 1977: 1183-4)

English (1977: 1183) indicates that *nang* is followed by the neutral form while *noon* may be followed by the imperfective form to connote an act that continues on for some time. As is clear from the examples above, *kung* is usually followed by the inceptive form, and (*ka*)*pag* by the imperfective. The question still remains as to whether (*ka*)*pag* precedes the perfective or the neutral form, although I glossed tentatively the verb forms as FN, as in (6a). Note also that English (1977,

1986) gives the following examples of (*ka*)*pag*, where (*ka*)*pag* precedes an imperfective form (8) or a perfective form (9).

(8) L-um-a-lápit  ang áso *kapág* t-in-a-táwag. (English 1977: 1184)
Ci-AV-UF-approach  SM  dog  when  Ci-PV-UF-call
'The dog comes when he is called.'

(9) *Kapág* na-tawíd   mo      na       ang ilóg, ikáw     ay
    when  PV.FN-cross 2SG.ng-A already SM river 2SG.NOM TM
    ligtás na.
    safe already
    'Once you cross the river, you are already safe.'     (English 1986: 961)

We are now in a position to explain another use of *kung*. *Kung* can also be used to introduce indirect interrogatives like 'if' or 'whether' in English, as seen below.

(10) a. Sabí-hin    mo         *kung* alín  ang gustó mo?          (BT: 84)
        say-IMP.PV 2SG.ng-A if       which SM  like 2SG.GEN/ng-A
        'Say which you like.'
     b. Alám       mo         ba *kung* kailán siyá      ba-balík?
                                                                  (BT: 84)
        know-UF.PV 2SG.ng-A Q if     when  3SG.NOM AV.NB-return
        'Do you know when s/he will return?'

English (1986: 961-2) indicates that *pag* can be used adverbially and is followed by root words, illustrating the following examples.

(11) a. *Pag* alís mo...
    when departure GEN/ng-A
    'When you leave, ...' or 'Upon your departure, ...'
  b. *Pag* ulán, ...'
    when rain
    'When it rains, ...'

Note, in addition, that *if* and *when* share some properties when they refer to events that may occur in the near future. They denote the *conditional* and express *time* in the near future.

(12) a. *Kung* ka-káin ka, mag-húgas ka ng
    if AV.NB-eat 2SG.NOM AV.IMP-wash 2SG.NOM ng-P
    kamáy.
    hand
    'If you eat, wash your hands.'
  b. *Kapág* walá' ka pa, i-íwan na
    if none 2SG.NOM still PV.NB-leave already
    kitá.
    1SG.ng-A:2SG.NOM
    'If you don't come, I will go alone.'
  c. *Kapág* t-um-akbó ka nang mabilís,
    if Ci-AV.FN-run 2SG.NOM ADVL fast
    ma-da-dapá' ka.
    AV-NB-stumble 2SG.NOM
    'If you run fast, you might stumble.'

### 27.3.2. *bagamán, káhit (na)*: **although**

(13) a. *Bagamán* mahína' ang katawán ni Lórna, k-in-áya
although weak SM body PN.SG.GEN Lorna Ci-PV.FN-able
pa rin niyá-ng t-um-áyo'.
still also 3SG.ng-A-LK Ci-AV.NT-stand up
'Although Lorna's body was weak, she could stand up.'

b. *Káhit na* marámi-ng táo, naká-lusót pa rin ang
although many-LK person AV.FN.able-get.away still also SM
magnanákaw.
thief
'Although there were a lot of people, the thief could get away.'

### 27.3.3. *dáhil (sa)*: **because (of)**

(14) a. *Dáhil* walá' pa-ng resúlta ang UPCAT, k-um-úha' pa
because none still-LK result SM UPCAT Ci-AV.FN-take still
ng ibá-ng eksám si Aura.
ng-P another-LK exam SM Aura
'Because the UPCAT's results have not come out yet, Aura took another exam.'
(UPCAT: University of the Philippines College Admission Test)

b. *Dáhil sa* ká-ta-talón mo, na-gibá' ang báhay
because of RF-RED-jump 2SG.ng-A PV.FN-break SM house
nátin.
1PL.INCL.GEN
'Our house fell down with your continuous jumping.'

It seems likely that *dahil* precedes a clause while *dahil sa* precedes a phrase or a word.

### 27.3.4. *samakatuwíd, kayá'*: therefore, so

(15) a. *Samakatuwíd,* táma' ang s-in-ábi ng títser ko
       therefore right SM Ci-PV.FN-say ng-A teacher 1SG.GEN
       tungkól sa kaniyá.
       about 3SG
       'Therefore, what my teacher told me about him/her is true.'

   b. Báta' pa siyá, *kayá'* hindí' pa siyá
      young still 3SG.NOM therefore not still 3SG.NOM
      t-in-anggáp sa trabáho.
      Ci-PV.FN-receive in work
      'He was still young, so he wasn't accepted for work.'

### 27.3.5. *káhit na*: even if

The conjunction *káhit na* 'although' also means 'even if'. The following are examples of *káhit na* that means 'even if'.

(16) a. *Káhit na* malakí ang suwéldo ko, kúlang pa rin.
       even if big SM salary 1SG.GEN insufficient still also
       'Even if my salary is high, it is not enough.'

   b. *Káhit na* marámi ka-ng péra, kung hindí' ka
      even if much 2SG.NOM-LK money if not 2SG.NOM
      namán masayá, bále-walá' rin.
      really happy worth-less also
      'Even if you have a lot of money, it is worthless if you are not happy.'

### 27.3.6. *bágo*: before

(17) a. *Bágo* ka um-alís, k-um-áin ka múna.
       before 2SG.NOM AV.NT-leave Ci-AV.IMP-eat 2SG.NOM first
       'Eat first, before you leave.'

  b. Gaw-ín mo itó *bágo* mo iyán
   do-IMP.PV 2SG.ng-A this.NOM before 2SG.ng-A that.NOM
   tapús-in.
   finish-NT.PV
   'Do this first before you finish that.' (gawín < gawa' + ín)

### 27.3.7. *pagkatápos*: after

(18) a. Um-iyák si Simón *pagkatápos* ng pelíkulá.
   AV.FN-cry SM Simon after GEN movie.film
   'Simon cried after the movie.'
  b. Na-túlog akó *pagkatápos* mag-labá.
   AV.FN-sleep 1SG.NOM after AV.NT-wash.clothes
   'I slept after washing clothes.'
  c. T-um-akbó ang kabáyo *pagkatápos* ng lában.
   AV-FN-run SM horse after GEN fight
   'After the match, the horse ran.'

In clauses, neutral forms often follow *bago* or *pagkatapos* without any specification of aspect. In phrases, genitive forms follow, as in (18a) and (18c). *Bágo* and *pagkatápos* denote temporal succession only. For spatial position, *sa harap ng* 'in front of' and *sa likod ng* 'at the back of' are used. This is different from languages such as Japanese, where the same forms have temporal and spatial senses.

# Chapter 28

# Verbal affixes

## 28.1. Introduction

Verbal affixes are used to derive verb forms from root words. This chapter deal with verbal affixes other than *-um-*, *mag-*, *-(h)in*, *-(h)an* and *ma-*.

## 28.2. *maki-* : request, joint/mutual action, etc.

The prefix *maki-* is agent-voiced, where it basically means 'to request the addressee to do something for the speaker/others'. Note, however, that Schachter and Otanes (1972: 333) indicate that: "derived verbs formed with the prefix *maki-* (plus; in some cases, other affixes) express actions that are performed together with another person or other people." See the following examples.

( 1 ) Maki-pag-báti' ka sa kaniyá.
AV.IMP-pag-greet 2SG.NOM with him/her
'Please make peace with him.'

(2) Naki-pag-úsap    kamí            sa    pári'  pára binyag-án
    AV.FN-pag-talk   1PL.EXCL.NOM    with  priest  for  baptize-NT.DV
    ang  anák                              namin.
    SM   child                             1PL.EXCL.GEN
    'We talked with the priest about baptizing our child.'

(3) Makí-ki-pag-úsap    kamí             sa    mga  opisyál   ng
    AV-NB-pag-talk      1PL.EXCL.NOM     with  PL   official  GEN
    gubyérno.
    government
    'We will have a dialogue with the government officials.'

(4) a. Naki-ki-káin   ng      hapúnan si     Ben sa    Nánay.
                                                    (Schachter and Otanes 1972: 333)
       AV-UF-eat     ng-P    supper    SM    Ben with  Mother
       'Ben is eating supper with Mother.' (mutual action)
    b. Naki-lígo'       kamí             sa    báhay  nilá.
       AV.FN-bathe     1PL.EXCL.NOM      LOC   house  3PL.GEN
       'We took a bath at their house.'
    c. Makí-ki-lúto'   silá             sa    kápitbáhay   nilá.
       AV-NB-cook     3PL.NOM          in/at neighbor     3PL.GEN
       'They will cook at their neighbor's house.'

## 28.3. *paki-*: request

*Paki-* is the PV counterpart of *maki-*. English (1986: 957) indicates that: "*paki-* is affixed to some verbs or root-words thereby connoting the idea of *kindly, please*", as illustrated by example (5).

(5) Paki-sábi      mo           sa kaniyá ang tungkól sa bágay na iyón.
                                                            (English 1986: 957)
    PV.IMP-say 2SG.ng-A to 3SG   SM  about      thing LK that
    'Please speak to him/her about that matter.'

It is worth mentioning that *ang* in (5) serves as a nominalizer and the form *ang tungkól sa bágay na iyón* serves as the subject.

(6) Paki-sábi    (mo)      sa kanilá na ma-hu-hulí akó        sa kláse.
    PV.IMP-say 2SG.ng-A to 3PL    LK  AV-NB-late 1SG.NOM in class
    'Please tell them that I'll be late for class.'

(7) Paki-línis     (mo)     namán ang mésa.
    PV.IMP-clean 2SG.ng-A also    SM  table
    'Please clean the table.'

(8) P-in-aki-táwag   ko         ang doktor sa kaniyá.          (BT: 69)
    Ci-FN-PV-call 1SG.ng-A SM  doctor to 3SG
    'I requested her to call the doctor (for me).'

In examples (7) and (8), the *ang*-marked NP functions as Patient. In (6), the clause headed by the linker *na* as a whole serves as the subject. Note, however, that *paki-* in (9) below expresses the action that will be done for *ako* 'I'. This use of *paki-* is benefactive-like, which may be related to the *ipaki-* form. A similar usage of *paki-* to (9) can be found in Aspillera (1969: 69), as seen in (10) below, where *báta'* 'child' is used as the patient to whom the ride is given.

(9) Paki-bilí     (mo)      akó        ng   mónay sa ibabá'.
    (?)IMP-buy 2SG.ng-A 1SG.NOM ng-P monay in downstairs

'Please buy me monay downstairs. (*Mónay* is a kind of soft bread.)

(10) P-in-aki-ki-sakáy      niyá        ang báta' sa áming    kótse. (BT: 69)
     Ci-PV-paki-UF-ride 3SG.ng-A SM child in 1PL.LK car
     'She requests us to give the child a ride in our car.'

## 28.4. *naka-* : stative

In Chapter 22, we discussed the prefix *naka-* in relation to *maka-* that is used to express ability, because they are formally similar.

(11) Naká-pálda siyá.
     STAT-skirt 3SG.NOM
     'She wears a skirt.'

(12) Naká-tsinélas ang báta'.
     STAT-sandal SM child
     'The child wears sandals.'

(13) Naká-reló    ang babáe.
     STAT-watch SM woman
     'The lady wears a watch.'

The prefix *naka-* is attached not only to nouns meaning clothes and accessories but also to nouns or verbal root words denoting actions.

(14) Ang áming       báhay ay   naka-tayó'   sa    may simbáhan.
                                               (English 1986: 1397)
     SM 1PL.EXCL.LK house TM STAT-stand in/at exist church

'My house is situated by the church.'

Note that the particle *sa* in (14) serves as a nominalizer and *sa may simbáhan* denotes 'in the place where the church is located'. As mentioned earlier, the particles *ang*, *ng* and *sa* in Tagalog can also be used as nominalizers, along with case markers. See also example (5) above.

## 28.5. *(i)pa-* : causative (patient-voiced)

(15) I-pá-húli        mo         ang  íbon.
     PV-CAUS-catch  2SG.ng-A  SM   bird
     'Ask someone to catch the bird.'

(16) I-pá-sáing       mo         ang  kánin.
     PV-CAUS-steam  2SG.ng-A  SM   cooked rice
     'Ask someone to cook the rice.'

When a causee is overt, it appears in the dative form.

## 28.6. *papag-* : causative (causee-voiced)

(17) Papág-igib-ín              mo          siyá        ng    túbig.
     CAUS-fetch.water-IMP.PV  2SG.ng-A  3SG.NOM  ng-P  water
     'Ask him/her to get some water.'

(18) Papág-walis-ín          mo          siyá.
     CAUS-sweep-IMP.PV   2SG.ng-A  3SG.NOM
     'Ask him/her to sweep (the floor).'

(19) Papág-turú-in       mo         siyá. (RW: *túro'*)
    CAUS-teach-IMP.PV  2SG.ng-A  3SG.NOM
    'Ask him/her to teach (class).

## 28.7.  *ka-* : recently finished 'just finish V-ing'

Here we take at another look at *ka-*, because it is attached to the form RED + RW, producing the verb form that means that an agent has just finished an action. As mentioned before, this type of construction has no *ang*-marked NP.

(20) Ka-ta-tápos       ko         lang  mag-luto'    ng      isdá'.
    RF-RED-finish   1SG.ng-A  just   AV.NT-cook  ng-P   fish
    'We have just finished cooking a fish.'

(21) Ka-li-línis       lang  námin            ng      báhay.
    RF-RED-clean  just   1PL.EXCL.ng-A  ng-P   house
    'We have just finished cleaning a house.'

(22) Ka-ra-ratíng        lang  ni             Tóny  gáling sa kláse.
                                                              (ratíng < datíng)
    RF-RED-arrive   just   PN.SG.ng-A  Tony   from        class
    'Tony has just arrived from class.'

# Chapter 29
# Nominal and adjectival affixes

## 29.1. Introduction

Nominal and adjectival affixes are used to derive nouns and adjectives from root words, respectively. In other words, these affixes are marked on root words, with the result being that nouns and adjectives are newly derived.

## 29.2. Nominal affixes

### 29.2.1. *ka-RW-an*: abstract noun

The form *ka-RW-an* usually derives abstract nouns from root words: e.g. *ka-gandá-han* 'beauty' from *gandá*. Observe the following examples.

(1) a. Magandá ang ka-tayú-an niyá sa búhay. (cf. *tayó*)
    beautiful SM stand 3SG.GEN/ng-A in life
    'Her status in life is OK.'
  b. Ma-ki-kíta nátin ang ka-sagút-an sa lángit.
    PV-NB-see 1PL.INCL.ng-A SM answer from sky
    'We can get the answer from the sky.'

c. Pag-ta-taním      ang  ka-buháy-an nilá.
   NML-RED-plant  SM     life         3PL.GEN
   'Their only means of living is farming.'
d. Malakí  ang    ka-ragát-an. (cf. *dágat*)
   big     NOM    ocean
   'The ocean is wide.'

The form *ragát* is derived from *dágat* via the morphphonemic rule $d \rightarrow r/V\_V$. It seems that in the *ka-RW-an* derivations, the stress shift occurs in more noun-like RWs, as in *ka-ragát-an* and *ka-buháy-an*, while it does not occur in more verb-like RWs, as in *ka-tayú-an* and *ka-sagút-an*.

### 29.2.2.   -*(h)an*: place

This suffix forms the noun meaning the place where the action denoted by a root word occurs, as shown by *upúan* 'seat, anything to sit on' derived from *upó* 'to sit'.

( 2 ) a. May  tindá-han sa  kánto.
        exist sell       at  corner
        'There is a <u>store</u> at the corner.'
    b. Marámi-ng  saging-án   sa  prubínsya.
       many-LK    banana      in  province
       'There are a lot of <u>banana plantations</u> in the province.'
    c. Kailán  ang  pasuk-án sa  UP?
       when   SM   enter    in  UP
       'When is the <u>first day of class</u> in UP?'
    d. Násaan  ang  labás-an sa gusáli-ng     itó? (*gusáli* 'building')
       where   SM   outside  in building-LK  this
       'Where is the <u>exit</u> in this building?'

### 29.2.3. *tag-* : related to weather or season
( 3 ) a. Tag-ulán na.
   in-rain   already
   'It is the rainy season now.'
   b. Tag-lamíg sa Hapón.
   in-cold   in Japan
   'It is winter in Japan.'

### 29.2.4. *ka-*
This prefix is attached to verbal root words, producing words that mean those who do the action denoted by the RWs. This prefix is an equivalent of the suffix *-er* in English *V-er*, as in *teach-er*.

( 4 ) a. Ka-túlong   si   María.
   person-help SM Maria
   'Maria is a helper/maid.'
   b. Síno ang ka-sáma     mo?
   who SM person-go.with 2SG.GEN/ng-A
   'Who is your companion?'

### 29.2.5. *pang-* : (used) for
( 5 ) a. Pang-línis ng   bányo   itó.
   for-clean ng-P bathroom this
   'This is used for bathroom cleaning.'
   b. Pam-pa-gandá     ang make-up.
   for-CAUS-beautiful SM make-up
   'The make-up makes one beautiful.'
   c. Pam-babáe itó.
   for-woman this

'This is for women.'

### 29.2.6. *maN-RED*: habit or occupation

This represents the habit or occupation related to the meaning of a root word, as seen below.

( 6 ) a. Mang-ga-gamót ang tátay ni Paéng.
   duty-RED-medicine SM father PN.SG.GEN Paeng
   'Paeng's father is a doctor.'
  b. Mang-i-ngisdá' si Paéng. (*isdá*': fish)
   duty-RED-fish SM Paeng
   'Paeng is a fisherman.'

*Mang-i-ngisdá*' is an irregular form, because *maN-RED-isdá*' would have produced the form *mang-i-isdá*'. (N is realized as [m], [n] and [ŋ], which are assimilated with the subsequent sounds.)

## 29.3. Other affixes: producing prepositional phrases

### 29.3.1. *taga₁-/tagapag-* : duty, assignment

( 7 ) a. Taga-labá ang nánay ko.
   duty-wash SM mother 1SG.GEN
   'My mother is a laundry woman or in charge of washing.'
  b. Tagapag-línis ng opisína si Kíko'.
   duty-clean ng-P office SM Kiko
   'Kiko is in charge of cleaning an office.'
  c. Taga-bása ng Gospel sa simbáhan si Aníta.
   duty-read ng-P gospel in church SM Anita
   'Anita is in charge of reading Gospels in the church.'

### 29.3.2. $taga_2$-: from

This affix is similar to the English preposition *from* and different from $taga_1$-. *Tagasaan ka ba?*, for example, can be translated into 'Where are you from?' Therefore, I transcribe this as **$taga_2$-**.

( 8 ) Taga-Batangas si Dexter.
from-Batangas SM Dexter
'Dexter is from Batangas.'

# References

Adams, Karen L. and Manaster-Ramer Alexis. 1988. Some questions of topic/focus in Tagalog. *Oceanic linguistics* 27: 79–101.
Aspillera, Paraluman S. 1969. *Basic Tagalog for foreigners and non-Tagalogs*. [BT] Tokyo: Tuttle.
Blake, Barry J. 1976. On ergativity and the notion of subject. *Lingua* 39: 281–300.
Blake, Barry J. 1994. *Case*. Cambridge: Cambridge University Press.
Bloomfield, Leonard. 1917. *Tagalog texts with grammatical analysis*. [TGA] University of Illinois. (Reprinted in 1967 by the Johnson Reprint Corporation.)
Bloomfield, Leonard. 1933. *Language*. London: George Allen and Unwin.
Bowen, J. Donald. 1965. *Beginning Tagalog*. Berkley and Los Angeles: University of California Press.
Bowen, J. Donald. (ed.) 1968. *Intermediate readings in Tagalog*. [IRT] Berkley and Los Angeles: University of California Press.
Campbell, George L. 1995. *Concise compendium of the world's languages*. London and New York: Routldge.
Castle, Cora Salvacion and Laurence McGonnell. 2000. *Teach yourself Tagalog*. London: Hodder and Stoughton.
Comrie, Bernard. 1981. *Universals and linguistic typology*. Oxford: Blackwell.
Constantino, Ernest A. 1970. The deep structure of Philippine languages. *The Archive* 1, No. 2: 65–79. Dept. of Oriental languages and Linguistics. Quezon City: University of the Philippines.
Constantino, Ernesto A. 1971. Tagalog and other major languages of the Philippines. In: Sebeok, Thomas A. (ed.), *Current trends in linguistics* 8 (*Linguistics in Oceania*): 112–154. The Hague: Mouton.
Constantino, Ernesto A. 2000. Current topics in Philippine linguistics. *Parangal cang Brother Andrew*. 57–68. Manila: Linguistic Society of the Philippines.
Davison, Alice. 1984. Syntactic markedness and the definition of sentence topic. *Language* 60: 797–846.
English, Leo James, C. Ss. R. 1977. *English-Tagalog Dictionary*. Mandaluyong City: National

Book Store.
English, Leo James, C. Ss. R. 1986. *Tagalog-English dictionary*. Mandaluyong City: National Book Store.
Foley, Willam A. 2008. The place of Philippine languages in a typology of voice systems. In: Austin, Peter K. and Simon Musgrave. (eds.), *Voice and grammatical relations in Austronesian languages*. 22–44. Stanford: Center for the Study of Language and Information.
Foley, William A. and Robert Van Valin, Jr. 1984. *Functional syntax and universal grammar*. Cambridge: Cambridge University Press.
Foley, William A. and Robert Van Valin, Jr. 1985. Information packaging in the clause. In: Shopen, Timothey. (ed.), *Language typology and syntactic description 1: Clause structure*. 282–364. Cambridge: Cambridge University Press.
Gil, David. 1993. Tagalog semantics. *BLS* 19: 390–403.
Guzman, Videa P. 1988. Ergative analysis for Philippine languages: an analysis. In: McGinn, Richard. (ed.), *Studies in Austronesian Linguistics*. 323–345. Ohio: Ohio University Center for International Studies.
Himmelmann, Nicholaus P. 2005. Tagalog. In: Adelaar, Alexander and Nicholaus P. Himmelmann. (eds.), *The Austronesian languages of Asia and Madagascar*. 350–376. London and New York: Routledge.
Hirano, Takanori. 2005. Subject and topic in Tagalog. *Papers of the Taiwan-Japan joint workshop on Austronesian languages*. 19–44. Taipei: Humanities Research Center.
Hirano, Takanori. 2007. Tagarogugo no settoozi *ma-* no kinoo to tadoosei (The functions of the prefix *ma-* in Tagalog and transitivity). In: Tsunoda, Mie, Kan Sasaki and Tooru Shionoya (eds.), *Tadoosei no tsuu-gengoteki kenkyuu* (*Cross-linguistic studies of transitivity*). 41–54. Tokyo: Kurosio.
Hirano, Takanori. 2010. Two types of topic construction. (Ms.)
Ishigaki, kenji. 1955. *Joshi no rekishiteki kenkyuu (Historical studies of case particles in Japanese)*. Tokyo: Iwanami.
Keenan, Edward L. 1985. Passives in the world's languages. In: Shopen, Timothy (ed.), *Language typology and syntactic description 1: Clause structure*. 243–281. Cambridge: Cambridge University Press.
Keenan, Edward L. and Bernard Comrie. 1977. NP accessibility and universal grammar. *Linguistic inquiry* 8: 63–100.
Kroeger, Paul. 1988. Verbal focus in Kimaragang. *Papers in Western Austronesian linguistics* 3: 217–240. Canberra: Pacific Linguistics. (A–78)
Kuroyanagi, Tetsuko. 1990. *Totto-Chan: Ang batang babae sa bintana*. [TC] Translated by Rosario Torres-Yu. Tokyo: Daido Life Foundation.
Li, Charles N. and Sandra A. Thompson. 1976. Subject and topic: a new typology of language.

In: Li, Charles N. (ed.), *Subject and topic*. 457–489.
Li, Charles N. and Sandra A. Thompson. 1981. *Mandarin Chinese: A functional reference grammar*. Berkley/Los Angeles/London: University of California Press.
McKaughan, Howard P. 1973. Subject versus topic. In: Gonzalez, Andrew B. (ed.), *Parangal kay Cecilio Lopez*. 206–213. Quezon City: Linguistic Society of the Philippines.
Moravcsik, Edith A. 1978. On the distribution of ergative and accusative patterns. *Lingua* 45: 233–279.
Nichols, Johanna. 1986. Head-marking and dependent-marking grammar. *Language* 62: 56–119.
Nolasco, Ricaldo. 2005. What Philippine ergativity really means. *Papers of the Taiwan-Japan joint workshop on Austronesian languages*. 215–238. Taipei: Humanities Research Center.
Payne, Thomas E. 1982. Role and reference related subject properties and ergativity in Yup'ik Eskimo and Tagalog. *Studies in language* 6: 75–106.
Pittman, Richard. 1966. Tagalog -um- and mag-: an interim report. *Papers in Philippine Linguistics* 1: 9–20. Canberra: Pacific Linguistics Series A–8.
Ramos, Teresita V. 1971a. *Tagalog dictionary*. [TD] Honolulu: University of Hawai'i Press.
Ramos, Teresita V. 1971b. *Tagalog structures*. [TS] Honolulu: University of Hawai'i Press.
Ramos, Teresita V. 1974. *The case system of Tagalog verbs*. Canberra: Pacific Linguistics.
Ramos, Teresita V. and Resty M. Cena. 1990. *Modern Tagalog*. [MT] Honolulu: University of Hawai'i Press.
Reid, Lawrence E. 2002. Determiners, nouns, or what? – Problems in the analysis of some commonly occurring forms in Philippine languages. *Oceanic Linguistics* 41: 295–309.
Schachter, Paul. 1976. The subject in Philippine languages: Topic actor, actor-topic, or none of the above. In: Li, Charles N. (ed.), *Subject and topic*. 491–518. New York: Academic Press.
Schachter, Paul. 1977. Reference-related and role-related properties of subjects. In: Cole, Peter and Jerrold Sadock. (eds.), *Syntax and semantics 8: Grammatical relations*. 279–306. New York: Academic Press.
Schachter, Paul and Fe T. Otanes. 1972. *Tagalog reference grammar*. Berkley/Los Angeles/London: University of California Press.
Shibatani, Masayoshi. 1988. Voice in Philippine languages. In: Shibatani, Masayoshi. (ed.), *Passive and voice*. 85–142.
Shibatani, Masayoshi. 1997. Gengo no kinoo to koozoo to ruikei (Language: its function, structure, and type). *Gengo Kenkyu* 112: 1–32.
Shibatani, Masayoshi. 1998. Voice parameters. In: Kulikov, Leonid and Heinz Vater. (eds.), *Typology of verbal categories*. 117–138. Tübingen: Niemeyer.
Shibatani, Masayoshi. 2009. Elements of complex structures, where recursion isn't: the case of relativization. In: Givón, Talmy and Masayoshi Shibatani. (eds.), *Syntactic complexity* (TLS:

85). 163–198. Amsterdam/Philadelphia: John Benjamins.
Siewierska, Anna. 1991. *Functional grammar*. London and New York: Routledge.
Smith, Jeniffer L. 2009. Phonological contrasts between nouns and verbs. (Ms. presented to the 72nd Kyushu University workshop on linguistics.)
Steele, Susan. 1978. Word order variation: A typological study. In: Greenberg, Joseph H. (ed.), *Universals of human language* 4: 585–623. Stanford: Stanford University Press.
Traugott, E. Closs. and Bernd Heine. 1991. *Approaches to grammaticalization* 2: 93–133. Amsterdam: John Benjamins.
Ushie, Kiyona. 1975. *Indoneshia-go no nyuumon (An introduction to Bahasa Indonesia)*. Tokyo: Hakusuisha.
Wolff, John U. 1973. Verbal inflection in Proto-Austronesian. In: Gonzalez, Andrew B. (ed.), *Parangal kay Cecilio Lopez*. 71–91. Quezon City: Linguistic Society of the Philippines.
The following are fairy tales that translated into Tagalog from which illustrative sentences are taken.
[Isang madaling-basahing aklat ng Ladybird. Manila: National Book Store]
   Si Jack at ang puno ng bitsuwelas.
   Si Red Riding Hood at si Goldilocks at ang tatlong oso.
   Si Snow White at ang pitong duwende.
   Si Tatlong Grap na lalaking kambing.

# Index

## A
A    101, 102, 105
accusative    3, 25, 101, 102
accusativity    25
adverbializer    170, 183
adverbs    129
affectedness    120
agent voice    81
agent voice (AV)    73
agent-voiced    73, 81, 120
ang    4
appositive    69
appositive RC    70
aspect    23
aspects    76
AV    2

## B
borrowed words    11

## C
causative construction    157, 159

Cebuano    154

## D
dative *sa*    161
double-subject construction    131
dummy *it*    37
dummy subject    193

## E
empty subject    37, 194
ergative    3, 25, 101, 102
ergative analysis    150
ergativity    25
existentials    33, 189

## F
focus-system    17

## I
ikáw    156
iri    151
itó    150
iyán    150
iyón    150

## L
length    10, 11

## M
meteorology    193
morphemes    47
mpty subject    57
multi-voiced    23, 25, 107
multi-voiced system    17

## N
nang-adverbs    184
nasaán    137
neutral    78
neutral form    74
ng-A    3, 4, 27, 65, 85
ng-P    3, 4, 27, 65, 85
nito    152
nominalization    33, 42, 46
nominalizations    198
nominalizer    44, 198, 211, 213

non-canonical constructions 36

## P

P    101, 102, 105
patient voice    85
patient-voiced    120
possessives    33, 189
possessor relativization    68
prepositional *sa*    161
PV    2

## R

reduplication    25, 76, 77, 196
relative adverbs    70
root words    47, 49

## S

S    101, 102, 105
saán    137
sentential adverb    184
stress    2, 10
subject constraint    66
subject-verb agreement    31

## T

topicalization    29
topic-subject construction    131

## U

unaccusative    117, 118

underlying structure    23
unergative    117

## V

voice    19, 20
voice variation    22, 66
voice variations    21
vowel deletion    89

## W

word order    18

## Z

zero suffix    88

【著者紹介】

## 平野尊識（ひらの たかのり）

〈略歴〉1947年12月20日、福岡市生まれ。1972年3月九州大学大学院文学研究科言語学専攻修士課程修了（文学修士）。1974年5月から1975年9月までフィリピン大学大学院言語学科に留学（文部省アジア諸国派遣留学生）。九州大学文学部助手、北九州大学外国語学部講師、助教授、山口大学人文学部助教授を経て、現在同大学教授。

〈主要著書・論文〉
「連濁の規則性と起源」『文学研究』71（九州大学、1974年）、「節の名詞化と補語の順序関係」『言語研究』102（1992年）、'Compound nouns of the type NVn in Japanese: Their formation and relationship to subject/topic'. *Gengo Kenkyu* 121（2002年）、'Relative clause formation: Toward a new typology'. 『日本語の分析と言語類型』（くろしお出版、2004年）、「タガログ語の接頭辞ma-の機能と他動性」『他動性の通言語的研究』（くろしお出版、2007年）。

# Tagalog Grammar  A Typological Perspective

| | |
|---|---|
| 発行 | 2012年2月14日 初版1刷 |
| 定価 | 15000円＋税 |
| 著者 | © 平野尊識 |
| 発行者 | 松本功 |
| 装丁者 | Eber |
| 組版者 | 中島悠子（4&4, 2） |
| 印刷製本所 | 株式会社 シナノ |
| 発行所 | 株式会社 ひつじ書房 |
| | 〒112-0011 東京都文京区千石2-1-2 大和ビル2F |
| | Tel.03-5319-4916 Fax.03-5319-4917 |
| | 郵便振替 00120-8-142852 |
| | toiawase@hituzi.co.jp　http://www.hituzi.co.jp |

ISBN 978-4-89476-549-8

造本には充分注意しておりますが、落丁・乱丁などがございましたら、小社かお買上げ書店にておとりかえいたします。ご意見、ご感想など、小社までお寄せ下されば幸いです。

## LANGUAGE IN PAPUA NEW GUINEA
Edited by Toru Okamura   8,000 yen +tax

## Analytic Dictionary of Abkhaz
Tamio Yanagisawa   28,000 yen +tax